AN ANGEL CALLING
by
Caroline Quigley

An Angel Calling

Connect with your Guardian Angel and the Archangels to create the life you would like to live

by Caroline Quigley

Dedication: For Teresa.

Thank you, for helping my soul find its true path. I will always be grateful.

Contents

Acknowledgements

My deepest, deepest gratitude to God my Creator and all the Heavenly Angels and Spiritual Guides, who helped me write this book. I thank you for your unconditionally loving, divine guidance and universal support.

My heartfelt thanks to my divine soul-mate and twin-flame, my wonderful husband Eoghan Quigley, for all his unconditional love and support; especially for drawing the beautiful Angel illustrations and book cover for "An Angel Calling". Also for helping me edit and typeset this book, I am very, very grateful. From the depths of my soul, I thank you Eoghan, for always being there for me no matter what and for seeing my true light. I love you more than words can ever express.

A big thank you to both my sisters, especially my twin sister Anne for always being there for me, and my younger sister Irma for believing in my work. Thank you also, to my Mother Ethna and brother Hendrik.

And a very special thanks to my nieces and nephew, Francesca, Hannah, Katie and Andre, for your beautiful unconditional joy and light.

My special thanks and Hugs to all of my close friends who have supported me down through the years and believed in me.

My very grateful appreciation and thanks to Grainne, Marguerite, Mary, Ethna, Frances, Vivian, Emer, Pauline, Helen,

Orla, Andrea and Eoghan for sharing your true Angel stories in this book.

My grateful thanks to Keith my Solicitor and Pat my Accountant, for all your help and guidance,

A big thank you to all the different therapists, clients, holistic and healing centres, who have supported me and my Angel work down through the years, I am so, so very grateful to you all.

Also many thanks to you, the reader, for buying this book.

Angel-Blessings and Light to you all,

Caroline Quigley.

Introduction

People often ask me when did I first start believing in angels? Well the truth is, I have always been aware of the presence of angels in my life. However, there were of course times of separation, when life became difficult and my soul went into a deep forgetful sleep, only to be reawakened again by the heavenly angelic realm.

Having been born a twin, two months premature in Dublin's Rotunda hospital, my twin sister an I were indeed very small babies. We were christened and blessed in the hospital. My Mother hoping that we would live and be well, which we did, we thrived and later on we moved to Holland with our parents. After a couple of years of living in Holland as a family, my parents decided when I was a toddler to move back to Ireland and settle in County Wicklow.

As a child I loved being out in nature, I vividly remember as early as three years of age, being out in the garden with my twin sister and feeling completely connected to everything around me, Mother Nature, the skies, flowers and trees. I could even sense and hear distant voices around us singing. Sometimes I used to see light filled beings around me; they seemed to be softly sparkling with a very bright white peaceful light.

These beautiful beings of light (Angels) seemed to move gracefully and in harmony together. They had a bright mist-like presence around them. I remember feeling very happy and joyous whenever they were near me.

As a child, I naturally wanted to discover everything. I was very inquisitive and intuitive; I had a fascination with nature, the sea, colours and light. I was also deeply creative, I read every book I could find, I loved music, dancing and singing. I even attended the local ballet school for ten years. Being left handed, I was always using the right side of my brain, the intuitive creative nurturing side (As most right handed people use the left side of their brain more frequently, the doing, practical, logical side etc). I however, was always in a world of beauty and enchantment, I felt constantly surrounded by angels and nature beings (fairies).

When I first started going to junior school, I used to often get a sense of colour and light around other children in my class. In my innocence, I thought there were rainbows around them, as back then I didn't realise that I was actually tuning into the aura (our very own individual energy field around the body). School held no interest for me, except when we were doing art, drama, or English. I also loved nature classes, where the whole class would go on a little nature walk.

Near our little junior school, there was a small grotto to Mother Mary that was up a little hill, surrounded by trees and an old chapel ruin. I loved it; it seemed to me to be a magical, mystical, heavenly place. I remember constantly asking my teacher if we could go there for our nature walk. For me it was sacred, a piece of heaven on earth, where I could connect with my angels, in my own child-like spiritual world. Every time our class went for a nature walk to the grotto, a little robin would appear serenading us with his song (to this day this still happens to me if I am out in nature, a little robin will nearly always appear). When it was time to go back to the class room, I often found it difficult to leave the memory of the grotto behind and face the reality of school again.

It was at this time, around the age of five or six that I became increasingly aware of my intuitive abilities and being able to pick up other people's energy. I would often get a sense of the nice or the mean girls in my class and I even knew what way my teacher was truly feeling. Also being a twin, I was naturally quite sensitive and very in tune with my twin sister, so this made it easier for me as a child to understand others on a deeper emotional level.

I remember very clearly one day, my Grandmother came to visit us. My Grandmother was a very kind woman who always wore nice hats and coats and brought us out little bars of Cadbury's chocolate. As I came into our kitchen "I could feel", my Grand- mother flinch on the chair as she was drinking her cup of tea. I intuitively went over and putting my hand on my Grandmother's right knee, I said "Grandma is your knee alright". A little taken aback, my Grandmother said "Yes love, how did you know that?" and then she laughed, good-humouredly. That day was the beginning of my sense of "knowing".

At my junior school, I remember an elderly, well meaning, kind nun, trying to encourage me to be right handed. I did try for a while to write with my right hand, but I began to develop a slight stammer. Then I naturally started to use my left hand to write with again and my stammer just simply disappeared. I now know it is very important to allow your body to flow naturally, if not this can often create blocks of fear, causing physical problems. As I gave up writing with my right hand and did what felt good and natural to me (writing with my left hand). I felt more in tune with my spirit and as a result my creative abilities just flowed and my stammer stopped.

A few years later, I started attending the local secondary school, and it was right there, that my nightmare began. My twin and I had gone from a lovely positive private little junior school, to a very large public secondary school, which was made up of several schools in the area. We were all streamed into four different classes. None of our friends from our old school were in our class; looking back, it was a lonely experience indeed. My twin and I must have been very easy targets for the school bullies, both of whom were in our class. We were twins, from an Irish Dutch background and we had come from a private little junior school to quite a big public senior school.

My twin sister and I were also extremely creative and sensitive. However this only seemed to make things worse, especially as I was sent up to the higher class for English. I loved English and I escaped really through my books and essays. In fact "I lived" for my English class, I guess it helped me find some kind of peace, but to the bullies I was the "goody girl". Most of my secondary school days, I lived in a distant haze, thankful for the support of my twin. I used to literally count the days to holidays and tried as often as I could to be sick, even skipping classes here and there, when my Mother was at work.

When I came home from school, I often felt very unworthy and unconfident, walking with my head down a lot of the time, which prompted some of the local children who lived near, to laugh and make fun of myself and my twin sister.

Things back then, seemed to go from bad to worse, as my father, who was a difficult, volatile, abusive man, left our family. My life then became a constant treadmill of being bullied at school and on the road where we lived, then coming home and trying to cope with my new family situation, amidst all the usual teenage angst and worries.

Looking back then, I guess I was very angry at God and my angels. As a teenager, I felt abandoned and ignored. It was then, that I decided to shut down (subconsciously) my intuitive abilities and my angelic connection. I moved swiftly away from my angels and it would take another fourteen years for my angelic connection to resurface again.

I decided at nineteen, two months before my twentieth birthday, to leave for London. I was hoping to pursue my creative talents. In London, I attended the academy drama school and did my Lamda exams. I went on then to study with the Lee Strasberg (method acting) institute, whilst juggling several menial jobs. At that time I was also involved, in a very negative, long-term relationship that eventually became quite soul destroying. When my relationship eventually ended, I felt emotionally drained and burnt out, so I returned home and settled in Dublin. In Dublin I spent most of my twenties being involved in the creative arts and helping run a small profit share theatre and film company.

By the time I was twenty seven, I had become physically unwell. I was exhausted, as I had not looked after myself down through the years, working in many different low paid jobs, whilst pursuing my artistic dreams. In all of my relationships I had been the giver, never knowing how to look after me. I had always been taking care of everyone else around me and now on top of it, things were not good financially for me either. No wonder my soul "subconsciously" cried out for help.

The angels must have heard my cry for help because a change was now imminent. Out of the blue, a work colleague at the time, told me of a well known holistic and spiritual healer called Teresa, so a little sceptical, I booked an appointment. I went to see Teresa for my appointment and I received some gentle healing with holistic massage. But it was during this treatment, that my life would truly change forever.

As I was receiving the healing from Teresa, a ray of pure white light seemed to flood in through the little window of the therapy room. I could sense this white light pouring down on me, filling up my mind and body with peace and healing, while at the same time comforting and supporting me.

I just knew in that moment, something very profound was happening. I felt a wonderful presence beside me and I instantly knew it was my Guardian Angel. I could sense my Guardian Angel, enfolding me very softly in its wings. I made a decision "to just be", and letting go, I relaxed back in my Guardian Angel's loving embrace.

Waves of unconditional love and healing light began to pour over me. I truly felt wonderful and I slowly began to realise how down through the years, I had let myself become completely disconnected from my angels.

As the memories started to come flooding back, I remembered my connection to the angels that I'd had as a child, also my intuitive abilities. When a feeling of unconditional love, peace and unity, started to sweep over me. I instantly felt healed, joyous and alive. It was as if I was walking on air. Even all my senses seemed to come alive, as if the dusty layer of denial was being removed.

After this beautiful spiritual healing experience, I had to re-evaluate my life and beliefs. I remembered as a child, I truly felt that God our Creator and all the Angels, were everywhere, all around us. I also knew deep in my heart that in spirit there is no separation, as we are all the same in the eyes of God our Creator. All we have to do is go deep within ourselves and connect to who we truly are in spirit and just be, (be still and know that I am God), to create that direct line to God our Creator and our Angels.

I now realised that my angels had never left me - I had left my angels, due to my own unhappiness, but how wonderful it was to reconnect again.

My soul now felt truly free and I was able to connect again spiritually once more with God and the Angels.

Later on I started to attend spiritual and positive living classes and I completed a holistic and spiritual healing course. I also started to pray and meditate daily with my Angels and I would often feel my angels' presence with me. I intuitively would receive little signs and messages from my angels, everything from finding small white feathers, to receiving cards or presents from people with angels on them. I even saw my prayers and requests being answered and little miracles happening in my life, such as my health and my inner happiness improving.

In the beginning after my re-awakening, friends and colleagues would often ask me to do angel healing work with them, or give them intuitive and spiritual guidance. I did enjoy doing that for a while, but a time came when I just had to accept that this part of my life was truly who I was in spirit. My soul was crying out for a change, so I left my safe office job in Dublin, and I moved over to the U.K. where I studied and completed several holistic angel courses, as well as meditation and flower essence diplomas.

Initially, I started doing some private angel healings and spiritual readings. But this then moved into more direct angel sessions, workshops and classes.

In 2005, myself and my husband, felt drawn to move back to the West of Ireland, where I have been living and working happily, as a holistic angel healer, spiritual intuitive and author. I do feel my heavenly Angels are always working with me, guiding me in my private angel sessions, workshops and classes. I thank God / Universe and all my beloved angels daily, for their unconditional love and assistance in my life, and in all my healing work.

Introduction

How this book came about:

In my private angel sessions, workshops and classes, people were always asking me, if I could recommend different angel information or meditations. So they could connect easily with their Guardian Angel and the Archangels.

Even though, I would always give general information on the angels to my clients, the demand for angel information became simply too much. As a spiritual intuitive, angel healer and holistic practitioner, there are only so many people you can see and classes you can teach, especially to do with energy or healing work.

So this book "An Angel Calling" was born, to help people connect easily and creatively with their angels. All the angel meditations and visualisations in this book I have channelled myself, in a loving, positive, spiritual way with the angels. In fact all the angel techniques in this book, I would use myself and in my workshops and classes.

"An Angel Calling", is also written from a universal, spiritual, unconditionally loving perspective. So absolutely anyone can read this book and work with their angels, regardless of background or beliefs. This book is for everyone, even if you are just tuning into your angels for the first time, you can read and work with this book.

The Angel hierarchy is very simply explained and you can work with your Guardian Angel or the Archangels, using the various Angel techniques, meditations and visualisations. I have tried to keep this book user friendly, simple, creative and inspirational, to bring you on your own individual journey of angel discovery.

"An Angel Calling", can help move you towards having the life you would like. By working and connecting with the Heavenly Angels, you can help manifest your dreams, sometimes even creating miracles along the way.

I have tried to keep "An Angel Calling", true to the work I do, and how I have experienced the presence of the angels in my life. I firmly believe that everyone can connect with their angels, if they really want to.

Through out the book, I have also included many true and inspirational angel stories. Some of the angel stories and angel experiences are from my own personal journey with the angels and some are angel stories as told to me, by family, friends, work colleagues and clients.

I thank you, for choosing this book "An Angel Calling" to read, and may you now enjoy connecting with your heavenly angels, in a joyous, spiritual, loving way.

Angel-hugs and blessings to you all,

Caroline Quigley.

Chapter 1

Angels are Everywhere

Throughout the centuries, various well known prophets, healers, intuitives, religious orders, visionaries and artists, all spoke about the presence of angels. They wrote in holy books, on scrolls, used art, painting, music, to convey to us that our heavenly angels are indeed with us, in fact all around us.

The simple truth being that we are never alone, as our heavenly angels are always by our side, helping and guiding us. Angels are in our homes, schools, colleges, work places, hospitals and businesses. Sometimes people can quite clearly get a sense of angels in places of beauty and peace, out in nature, in libraries, galleries, churches, temples and meditation centres. All we have to do is simply believe that these heavenly messengers are there to support and guide us.

But who or what are angels? For some people angels are heavenly protectors or messengers, spiritual beings representing goodness and light. For others angels are joyous, fun, loving beings with cupid like images. Even down through the ages, angels were often seen as a symbol of miracles.

In truth, angels are all of the above and more, much more. In fact, quite simply put, "angels are beautiful beings of light created in the mind of God our Creator". Angels also have an ability to move at the speed of light, giving help and support to everyone in need. Therefore the angels are really "God's heavenly messengers", with their own unique talents and gifts.

What do angels look like? I often get asked this question, to be very honest, angels can vary in shape and size. Our own individual angel, known, as our Guardian Angel, can look just like you and I, often radiating a divine heavenly presence or light around them, known as the aura. Artists who were sensitive to the presence of angels often drew the aura in paintings as a halo of light.

Archangels however are very vast and tall angels with a very golden, light-filled presence. In the heavenly realms, some of the angels are very tall indeed. One thing all of the angels have in common is that they radiate pure unconditional love (When connecting with the Archangels during my work, I often see streams of golden light around the person or group I am working with).

Sometimes certain sensitive people can see or sense their angels working with them (these are indeed gifted and intuitive people who work with their senses). People have also told me, that they often get a sense of peace, calm, or light filling the room when their Guardian Angel is present, or just a feeling that they are being looked after.

Why are angels here? The answer is simply that angels have always been here, since the beginning of creation (angels are created by God Our Creator). In fact the angels' main task is to work within the heavenly spheres, though some of the angels such as the Archangels and our Guardian Angels in particular are sent to watch over and guide us.

Angels are definitely here to help us, as we go on our own individual journey throughout life. Angels can act as spiritual messengers and are said to form the bridge between heaven and earth, so we can easily connect with the Heavenly Realms. I feel that our angels are "the spiritual postmen and women, delivering our prayers and requests to God".

What does the word Angel mean? The word Angel comes from the Greek word "Angelo's", the translation being: "messenger of God or Light". It is very important to know that our heavenly angels will always work on our behalf. The only thing we have to do is to ask the angels for help or guidance by using our free will (the right to choose to ask for help or not). However our angels will never interfere in our lives unless we ask them to, as they are governed by the law of free will (one of God's Universal laws) which we as human-beings all have.

The only exception is: if we are in a dangerous situation (and it is not yet our time to leave the earth) or if we are constantly being led astray and going down the wrong path and there is no room for our soul to grow. Then in such extreme situations, the angels will often rush in to intervene without being asked. For example: if someone couldn't leave a bullying relationship, no matter how hard they tried and they had learnt all they could from that relationship for their soul's growth, the angels will then often create new options for the person to move on, often in a miraculous way. This always happens of course in divine timing (which is God's timing).

What do angels want from us? Angels do not want or need anything from us. As perfect beings, they live in a beautiful light filled world of love and miracles. However part of the angels' mission is to help us, so the only thing they are eager to do, is to genuinely help and support us.

Over the last thirty years, more and more people are becoming aware of angels. In fact the veil (the thin covering that separates us) between heaven and earth is getting thinner, as people start to raise their individual awareness of heaven and earth. As a result, the angels can now easily come to the earth to work with us. The more we connect with our heavenly angels, the more we can improve our feelings and energy vibration for the better, thus creating a more loving world for ourselves and others.

As human beings on the earth, we are always given the choice to work with the angels or not. It is simply up to us (free will). We can work with the angels through many different forms: prayer, meditation, writing, music, song, invocations, requests, affirmations, or by simply talking to our angels.

When we call upon our angels, rest assured that the angels will only work for our highest good, radiating pure unconditional love and creating miracles in our everyday lives. The important thing to remember is that the angels treat everyone equally, as we are all the same in the eyes of God our Creator.

Angels will always work on your behalf when called in or asked, but be aware that angels never ever partake in anything negative or underhanded. They simply wouldn't know how, as they only work in the light of God our Creator, in a loving positive way for the highest good of all.

We must also remember that we are working with highly developed, light filled spiritual beings. So it is important that when we invoke the angels, we do so with love, respect and gratitude. This creates a healthy connection between us, as the angels truly are our spiritual friends here on earth.

As human beings, we mainly work with our Guardian Angel and the Archangels. But Angels do also exist in the heavenly realms and they do have a certain order or hierarchy between them. This order is often called the "heavenly spheres" or levels of creation.

Heavenly Spheres:
Sphere 1)
Seraphim and Cherubim Angels

Seraphim and Cherubim Angels are in the highest group order, or 1st sphere in the heavens.

Seraphim Angels

Seraphim Angels are vast angelic beings of light, surrounded in a flame of divine love. They are said to sing praise and glory to God our Creator and are known as the singing angels (the heavenly voice or choir of angels).

Often people who have had near death experiences or have come close to death or experienced a miraculous healing, have reported hearing the Seraphim Angels singing.

Cherubim Angels

Cherubim Angels are very large tall angels and are often called the keepers of all that is light. The Cherubim Angels are said to watch over the sun, moon and stars, helping radiate this light all around the universe and down onto planet earth.

Sphere 2)
Thrones, Dominion, and Virtue Angels
Throne Angels:

Throne Angels are very powerful angels, often ruling over an individual planet. Our own planet earth is said to have its own individual throne angel, watching over and guiding it. Throne angels help carry out God our Creator's Divine Will and are also said to be the angelic messengers of balance and justice across the universe (including Heaven and Earth).

Dominion Angels:

Dominion Angels are said to have all dominion over the groups of angels that are under them. They bring light and infinite mercy, whilst often guiding, helping, enlightening and teaching other angels. Dominion angels can help to carry out God our Creator's intentions.

Virtue Angels:

Virtue Angels are often known as the angels of miracles. They send divine light and energy to the earth helping and inspiring many people. They work closely with our Guardian Angels and Archangels.

Sphere 3)
Powers, Principalities and Archangels
Powers:

The Power Angels, as the name suggests are quite simply powerful protectors. They protect us (our souls) against negativity on the earth, working in conjunction with Archangel Michael (the heavenly protector). They help keep us on the right track for our soul's journey here on earth. The Power Angels can also help us, by over seeing births, deaths and re-birth in our lives.

Principalities:

The Principalities are extremely tall Angels that look after countries, towns, cities, organisations and even world leaders. They are often seen as the angelic guards on the Earth.

Archangels:

The Archangels are powerful light filled angels, radiating a golden light or aura. They each have their own unique talents. Archangels work in conjunction with our Guardian Angels to help and support us here on the earth.

The four main Archangels are: Archangel Michael (fire), Archangel Gabriel (water), Archangel Raphael (air) and Archangel Uriel (earth).

Sphere 4)
Guardian Angels:

Guardian Angels are our own individual angels that are assigned to us when we are born. They are always with us on the earth, helping and guiding us. They are our helpers and best friends. They often keep us safe from harm and constantly help enlighten us.

Sphere 5)
Fairies and Elementals:

Quite simply the Fairies and Elementals are the angels of nature. These angels (fairy nature beings) work closely with Mother Nature and the natural environment. They are small, beautiful, light-filled, energetic, beings, gentle, yet fun and they help nature to grow and flourish.

As human beings, we mainly work with our Guardian Angels and the Archangels. You can of course work with the Angels from the heavenly realms or spheres. Although it is important to remember that all of these Angels have very definite roles in creation. Unless it is absolutely necessary (for example, asking for world peace or important planetary change) it would be quite disrespectful to ask the heavenly spheres of Angels for something mundane (such as help to pay your general household bills).

That's why our Guardian Angels are sent here to us on the Earth. Although even if you did ask the heavenly spheres of Angels (to pay your bills) nine times out of ten your Guardian Angel will be sent to intervene on your behalf. The heavenly spheres of Angels are just simply too busy sustaining all of God's Creation. Angels of the heavenly spheres have their very own talents and abilities especially designed for them to work with all of creation, just like we have our own talents and abilities as human beings.

Sometimes, when I give an overview of the angel hierarchy, I can be asked about negative angels, or fallen angels. To be very honest, this is not something I give much focus to. If a negative entity (non-spiritual being) is "fallen" or negative, it is quite simply not an angel.

Heavenly Angels are beings of Divine (God our Creator's) Light and unconditional love; they are God's messengers and helpers. Heavenly Angels only radiate peace, goodness and support. Angels do not have human nature, so they only know and give pure unconditional love.

Therefore a negative entity (or negative energy) or fallen angel, is never ever a Heavenly Angel. Negative entities are not from God our Creator. They can often even stem from our own fears or negative human emotions (ego, jealousy, hate, violence, anger etc) the residual energy of which can often even lay dormant above us in the atmosphere and affect our energy or aura from time to time.

That is why it is always important to clear our own energy (chapter 3) and to stay positive and in the light, feeling connected to God our Creator's unconditional love and light at all times.

If you ever feel worried or fearful, you can ask Archangel Michael and your Guardian Angel to work with you. Archangel Michael is our protector Angel on the earth and will remove any negativity or fears. Helping you stay in the light of God, in a loving balanced way, ensuring safety and peace around you.

We must remember that light attracts light, while negativity attracts negativity. So do try to choose, to be in the light as much as possible and please don't give destructive fears, such as negative energy or entities, superstitions, negative belief systems, any of your thoughts or power. Just simply try and walk the path of the light, with God our Creator and the Divine Heavenly Angels, then all will be well.

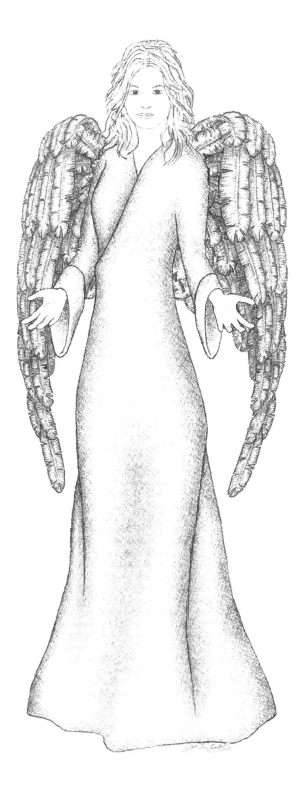

Chapter 2

Guardian Angels

Guardian Angel: Your Guardian Angel is your personal friend and helper on the earth. Assigned to us when we are born, our Guardian Angel protects and guides us on our life's journey.

Description: Our Guardian Angel radiates a beautiful pure divine white light. Guardian Angels are often described as beautiful and tall, radiating a serene presence. People can often see their guardian angel in a white gown of light with very large white or creamy wings.

Aura: Clear, pure white, divine light.

Colours: White, ivory, cream.

Symbol: A pure white feather, a rainbow, a ray of white light, an orb or circle of white light.

Animal: White butterflies, white doves, unicorns.

Crystals: Angelite and celestite.

Angelite: is a tumbled (smooth) form of celestite. It is very pale blue with cloudy pale markings. Angelite is said, to be the crystal of your Guardian Angel.

Celestite: is a deep silvery light blue, crystal rock formation, which is normally found in bed clusters, crystal points or geode form. Celestite is said to connect you to the celestial realms.

Flower Essence: *Star of Bethlehem:* it is supportive, soothing, comforting, helping remove sorrows and alleviates worries.

Working Together: Your Guardian Angel is your special guide, along your spiritual path in life. You can ask your Guardian Angel to help you with literally anything, as nothing is too big or small for your angel.

Your Guardian Angel often works in harmony with the various Archangels, to help bring about your requests or desires.

Often people turn to their Guardian Angel in times of need or hardship, by asking their angel to comfort them.

Your Guardian Angel, when asked, will always enfold you in their heavenly wings.

Our Guardian Angel is our angel that watches over us. Some people prefer to call their Guardian Angel, a spiritual best friend. It doesn't really matter the name, as your Guardian Angel is always with you.

When we are born, an angel is assigned to us, to welcome us onto the earth. This angel is our Guardian Angel. Our angel is with us at every stage of our development and guides us on our life's path. In fact our Guardian Angel stays with us until it is time for us to leave the Earth, then gently guiding us into the next life.

Guardian Angels can also be our protectors, as many times in our lives our angel can keep us out of harm's way. Our Guardian Angel is also our guide and teacher in life showing us where to go and what to do and is always working for our highest good.

We must remember that we as human beings have free will (choice), so we can ask our angels for their help and guidance. When we ask our Guardian Angels for help, they will always respond to our requests. As I said earlier, our angels do not inter- fere unless we ask them, the only exception being, if we are in danger or constantly going down the wrong path in life, then they may rush in to correct the situation.

You can confide in your angel about anything, as your Guardian Angel is very discreet and loves you unconditionally. Angels do not judge you, as they do not have that capacity (we are the only ones who can do that).

Angels do not have human nature; all they know is pure, unconditional love. As I said before, our angels are created in the perfect, infinite, loving mind of God our Creator. Therefore, our Guardian Angels are constantly radiating unconditional love and light to us here on the earth.

People often say to me, that they are unable to hear or sense their Guardian Angel and wonder why they can't connect with their angel. The first thing I often ask is, "have they actually talked to their angel or invited their angel in to work with them?" and the answer is often a resounding "no, they haven't". Well, your angel can't work with you or help you unless you ask them to. When you do ask, then your angel will always help and work lovingly with you.

Often I hear, "Well I did ask my angel to work with me but I couldn't hear, see, or feel my angel." Let me reassure you, that if you ask your Guardian Angel to work with you, your angel will always do so. In fact as soon as you call your angel in, you will start to notice that things begin to improve. It may just be subtle at first, but eventually there will be a change for the better. Even if you just feel more peaceful, take it as a sign that your angel is with you.

It can often take time to form a deep connection with our Guardian Angel. Sometimes people cannot feel or hear their angel, because they are not used to it and are simply unable to still their minds or there may be a lot of stress or negativity around them.

One thing we do need to be aware of is that angels do not care for destructive noise or negative vibrations. "Be still and know that I am God" was said for a reason, as angels were created in the mind of God. Therefore an angel's natural state is one of serenity, peace and love. Therefore dense, heavy or negative energy can make it hard for us to tune into the angelic realm.

My advice is, to spend a few moments in the peace somewhere, whether it's at home, in a quiet area or room, your garden, out in nature, or in a peaceful positive church or temple or meditation centre, all are good places to connect with your guardian angel.

Angels also love peace, natural sun-light, candles, beautiful music, serene surroundings, colour, flowers, statues, crystals, oils. All of the above are a great way, to help us invoke a spiritual ambience, so that we feel prepared to work with our angels.

If you ever feel a little negative, you may have absorbed some negative energy. So I would suggest, maybe having a nice clearing shower or a bath; sea salt is especially good for this. The Dead Sea salts (from the Dead Sea) are a wonderful reviver, as they help clear away any negativity and are a great way to detoxify as well.

I love the Dead Sea salts; they have often been described as the angelic sea salts because they are so pure. Along the Dead Sea the energy it is very healing and peaceful. The Dead Sea stretches from Jordan to Israel and down to the West Bank. It is said the Great Healer and Mystic Jesus Christ, walked along on the Dead Sea. The Dead Sea is also said to be frequented by angels.

Even walking by a sea shore can also be very clearing, as can eating healthy foods and drinking healthy juices and smoothies. When we drink pure water it can help restore our body and mind, helping all our organs function more efficiently. Water is a great healer and can boost our bodily systems; therefore pure water is one of the essences of life.

It is also important to do some form of exercise, as even gentle movement or walking can help us feel more positive. Our thoughts can also really help us physically and emotionally, as positive thoughts and thinking are known to literally lift our energy up, helping us shift into a better feeling vibration or frequency.

The reality is, we all can absorb negativity from time to time (we just have to switch on the news to feel bad) especially if we are sensitive or aware, but the angels can always help us to move back into a more positive and light filled world. Even in the midst of noise or chaos, our angel will always work with us and come to help us.

Remember your Guardian Angel is always by your side. You are never alone.

Chapter 3

How to work with your Guardian Angel

Sometimes when clients first come to see me they often ask "How can I work with my guardian angel?" I say to them that "you can work with your Guardian Angel anywhere and at anytime" and that "you can also talk or pray to your angel about anything you like", as the angels will always be at your side, working for your highest good.

There will be times in our lives that our Guardian Angel can not intervene, especially if we are meant to learn from a situation, as learning can often move us forward for our own personal growth. In these situations especially if it has been a trying time, take note that your Guardian Angel will still be with you, comforting and consoling you in the background as you learn and move forward.

I feel, to create the best results, it's important to contact your Guardian Angel in a loving, preferably peaceful setting (though your angel will always work with you regardless of the surroundings, even if there is noise etc. It can also be good, to clear away any clutter, so you have a more open, loving space. As this will help you connect to your Guardian Angel in a spiritual, relaxed way. But most of all its important to be with your angel, where ever you feel comfortable and at ease.

We must remember that our angels are light filled, joyous beings. So it is important to be positive with our angels, as joy, peace and happiness can help us connect easily to the angels and God our Creator.

People often tell me, that when they feel relaxed or happy they can hear, feel, or attune to their angel's presence very easily. At certain times though we may find it hard to connect to our angel, but please be aware that certain fears, negativity and even ego, can sometimes hold us back.

But no-matter what we are feeling at the time, our Guardian Angel will always be there at our side. All we have to do is trust and believe.

Clearing your Space

1) First of all, find a peaceful space or room that feels right for you to work in with your Guardian Angel.

2) Make sure the space is relatively clean, tidy and not cluttered.

3) Open the window or door of the space for a few minutes, let some fresh air in and make sure the room is warm, yet airy.

4) You may also like to clear the energy and purify the space, making it is easier for you and your angel to work together. Some people like to use a white sage smudge stick (available in most health shops or holistic shops). Burning white sage is an old technique used in the past by the Native American culture (Native Americans believed that white sage, purified an area dissolving any negativity or negative spirits).

My advice to you is to just use a very small amount of white sage, as too much can be overpowering. Take a small piece of white sage leaf, light it and blow out the flame. Place it on a plate and walk slowly around the room with it.

You may like to say: **"Dear God our Creator and all the Angels, bless this room, let only Divine Light enter this room now. Thank you, amen."** (It is important to thank, as this shows that you have confidence in the divine order of things).

5) You may then like to position your chair if sitting or if lying down, make sure your head is slightly raised up with a pillow (if you can) or you may drift off to sleep.

6) Sometimes flowers or pictures are nice as they brighten the room; though always try to choose positive themes or light filled colours.

7) You might like to create an ambience with candles, room oils, angel sprays, or have an angel statue present (however that is up to your own individual taste). Also candles do create a loving atmosphere bringing in the symbol of love and light (A candle's flame is natural light).

I would say try and avoid florescent or very bright lamps as this can often be distracting, however if you work with your angels in the evening a low lamp is fine.

8) Some people like to use a salt lamp, which are often orange in colour. This type of lamp is formed from natural rock salt. A very small light bulb is placed inside the salt lamp giving off a distinctive orange golden glow. Salt lamps are very comforting, as the salt deionises negative energy in the room, creating a lovely earthy atmosphere.

9) A small bowl of warm water with a few drops of lavender, or chamomile, can also leave the room smelling nice and relaxed.

10) You also may like to have soft blanket to hand if you feel cold or you need to be comfortable.

11) When working with your angel you might like to tell others not to disturb you or if you can, turn off your mobile phone.

Many people tell me that they like to have a little altar to work with their Guardian Angel, as this often helps them connect easily to the angels. Angel altars are wonderful as they create a sacred ambience in your space whilst giving you a spiritual place, to put your written requests, angel statues and candles.

Creating an Angel Altar

1) The first thing to do is to make sure that your space is clear and clean before you set up your altar.

2) Then find a table you like. It can be any type of table; wood is always more grounding and earthy then plastic, glass or steel (I like a round table as this represents wholeness, harmony, infinity and balance). A small to medium sized table is fine. Always make sure that your table is strong enough to stand up as an altar holding up your statues, candles etc. If you do not have a table a sturdy box or even open shelf could also be used.

3) Now wipe down the table and sprinkle a few drops of jasmine oil around it (or else your favourite oil). Jasmine is often called the oil of the angels; in many churches and temples, they often have jasmine burning.

4) Find a light coloured piece of material (white, ivory, cream etc) to cover your altar.

5) You might like to place an angel statue on the altar. You may also like to place a picture of an angel or a spiritual master or saint, or a spiritual figure you identify with on the altar (that's up to you).

6) A medium sized candle is good to place in the middle of the altar, any colour is fine, however white, cream, ivory and pale blue are the colours associated with your Guardian Angel. Always make sure your candle is able to stand up straight and the candlewick is not to long.

7) Flowers can bring a loving natural ambience and can be placed in a vase, or even scattered (roses or rose petals work best for this) on the altar.

8) Certain crystals work very well on the angel altar; angelite or celestite are good crystals to work with as it attunes you to your guardian angel. Clear quartz crystal (for healing), amethyst (for protection), rose quartz (for love) are good also. Often people like to place a crystal at each corner of the table, which is fine except if the table is round, then just place the crystals according to what feels right for you at the time.

9) Having a small bottle of holy water or healing well water or an angel spray, (many are available now in holistic centres and health shops), to place on the altar, or even spray around, helps to invoke a spiritual atmosphere.

10) I like to put, a small bowl or box on the table containing my requests or prayers.

11) A nice touch is for you to have a small white feather to put on the table, as a symbol of your Guardian Angel.

12) It is also nice to have angelic or beautiful music playing (Mozart and Bach were both inspired by the angels).

13) You may like to have hanging chimes or a Tibetan singing bowl which creates a beautiful deep hollow melodic sound, which vibrates around the room. Both are very uplifting and cleansing.

Now you are ready to move forward and work with your angel.

Before you start working with your angel, it is important to feel relaxed and at peace. As certainly a positive comfortable light filled space can help, but having a peaceful mind is the true key. This can be cultivated through gentle meditation.

I now enclose a simple meditation technique to help you feel relaxed and peaceful, as you prepare to work with your Guardian Angel.

*Please note: (all meditations and visualisations should not be done whilst driving or operating machinery).

White Candle Meditation

1) Light a white candle beside you, or whatever candle is on your altar (even a tea-light is fine, just as long as you can see the candle flame).

2) Then sit in a comfortable chair with your back as straight as possible, your feet firmly on the ground.

3) Visualise tiny little flowers coming down from the soles of your feet, pushing through the floor then connecting you to Mother Nature (so your feet feel grounded and safe).

4) Then if possible, quietly observe the white blueish flame of the candle. At first it may seem hard, but as you become accustomed to the candlelight it gets easier. (Watch the candle flame flicker and dance in a joyous way).

5) Close your eyes, and visualise yourself breathing in this pure light. Let this light fill your mind, body and spirit, and as you breathe out, breathe out any worries or anxieties. See them literally floating away and dissolving.

6) Let this light fill every part of your being, relax into it. You can also say a keyword: such as "peace", "calm", "love" or "goodness", as you breathe in the light.

7) Sense this white light all around you, starting now to fill up the whole room; it's so peaceful and serene.

Now you are ready to invoke your Guardian Angel.

Chapter 4

How to Invoke your Guardian Angel to work with you

Some people think that invoking or talking to their Guardian Angel has to be complicated. In fact nothing could be further from the truth, as invoking your angel is a natural, simple and easy process. As human beings we often tend to complicate things, believing that if it's not hard work or difficult, then something must be wrong, or we are not doing it properly. Sometimes when we try too hard, we can get into control (our ego) and then we tend to upset the balance or push the good away from ourselves, thus creating stress.

It's important to remember, that making contact with your angel should always be an easy and effortless process, as natural as breathing or sleeping, as our Guardian Angel is always with us. We just have to reach out and ask our angel to help us, and our angel will instantly come to our side and be there.

When you are finished speaking to your angel, try and let go of your request. Hand everything over to your Guardian Angel, then detach and just trust that everything is in the hands of the Divine. (This is very important because if we hold on to tightly to our prayer requests or desires, then we often block the result with our fears and rigid thinking.)

Remember our Guardian Angel only works in a positive loving way for our highest good. So let go, trust your angel, and go with the flow of life.

Always remember to thank your angel.

To Invoke your Guardian Angel:

You can simply say:

"Guardian Angel, be by my side."

"Blessed Guardian Angel, work with me now."

"I invoke thee now my Guardian Angel, to light and guide my way today."

"Guardian Angel, light my way."

Thank you.

(It is also important to say whatever feels right for you at the time).

Asking directly:

"My Guardian Angel, I ask you to work with me to-day, help me with............" (State your request or prayer).

"My dear Angel, I ask that................." (Just talk to your angel, like a best friend and ask for what you need). Thank you.

Affirmations:

"Guardian Angel, help me to feel well and positive today."

"Beloved Angel, open the way for many miracles today, let me receive...."

"Dear Guardian Angel, shower me with love and healing."

"My dearest Angel, send financial help and abundance today."

(Thank you, Amen).

Requests to our Guardian Angel:

Our requests are our special prayers or wishes that we hand over to our Guardian Angel. Some people like to write their request out, somewhat like a letter to their angel, or in point form, and place it on their angel altar or in a church. Others like to burn their request after writing it, even burying it in the ground or placing it in water. All of these techniques are good, creating a significant spiritual shift, which can allow an improvement to take place in our lives.

Request cards:

Request cards are a simple yet creative spiritual process, which involves writing to your angels.

1) Find a plain piece of A4 medium thick card or paper or a nice greeting card (white, Ivory, cream, is nice for your Guardian Angel). Then fold it in half (make it A5 size).

2) To make it your own, you may like to sprinkle a few drops of jasmine aromatherapy oil on it or perhaps some of your perfume. You can even bless it in the fresh air. Just do whatever feels right for you at the time.

3) On the outside of your card write your name, and the date and the time that you start writing your requests. A good time to write your angel request card is at seven am or seven pm. The number seven is a very spiritual number that corresponds to the angels, If you are unable to write your card at this time you can bring the number seven in on the minute for example: seventeen minutes past three or one forty seven and so forth.

(I feel at the hours of seven am or seven pm, closer to my angels. It may have to do with the time of the sun rising and setting nearer to seven. It is also said that multitudes of angels flock to the earth at this time to sing and praise God our creator's glory. We must also remember that there are seven main angelic realms (as discussed in chapter 1). Also the number seven has long been associated in Ireland, with healing, which is where the "seventh son of the seventh son" originates from. As most sons who are the seventh born, are often traditional healers and can perform the laying on of hands with great results.

Wise people down through the ages have said that there are seven stages related to our soul's growth, as we can reach different stages of growth here on the earth. Stage one and two are very basic living and learning stages, however as we move into stages three to four on the earth we can attain certain enlightenment. Therefore people who are at stage five are indeed very holy people on the earth and they normally project a very gentle, serene, evolved presence, as they are almost completely devoid of their ego and are helpful and kind. Stages six and seven are levels which we as human beings can only learn and attain in the heavenly realms when the time is right).

4) When I write to my angel I like to have nice soft music in the background with candles lighting. I also leave the window slightly open to bring in the light and Mother Nature.

5) Before you start, the important thing to remember is to write from your heart. Talking to your angel a bit like a best friend; as I've said before, many people like to write their requests in point form or as a letter. It is entirely up to you, whatever works best for you at the time. I would suggest that you write your requests in a peaceful positive way. You may like to play uplifting, gentle music, or just relax and take a few gentle deep breaths, or use the candle meditation (chapter 3).

6) Really think about what you want to ask your angel for and write from the heart.

It is important to work with your angel in the now, as the now creates your future. You are manifesting your future in a loving positive way alongside your angel. If you are not sure whether something is right for you, (for example, a certain relationship or career path) just express to your Guardian Angel, how you feel and then hand your requests over, always asking your angel to do what is right for you.

Our angels can often inspire us, helping open the way for a wonderful new beginning in our life. The angels can put different signs our way, for example you may get a strong feeling to open a book, or a newspaper, or look something up on the internet, go to a party, join a group or do an activity that you enjoy.

In fact angels can lead you to the right job, the right relationship and to people who can help and inspire you. All we have to do is ask and believe in our angels. It is also very important to let our requests or wishes go, without resistance, letting our angels deliver our requests to God our Creator, so they can heal and manifest into form with wonderful results.

7) Before I start writing my request card, I often say a little prayer and thank God our Creator and my angels for their unconditional love and support. I then take a couple of gentle deep breaths and I start to write.

I normally write a few different requests (but often one of my requests may take up an entire card). If you fill up your card, you can always put a few sheets of paper inside your card to write on as well, but keep the extra paper inside the card.

8) I would write:

"Dear Guardian Angel, I would like you to help me with (describe what you need)." Then I would thank the angels and sign my name. Remember here, that your signature is important, as it is your own individual stamp. It's saying to your angel "here is my request card", and by the action of thanking, letting go and signing your request card, it's giving your angel permission to work on your behalf.

9) When writing your request out to the angels, do try and be clear about what you really want and then write your request in as much detail as possible. I always say keep it honest, real and be yourself, as this is why your angel loves you so very much.

10) Once you have finished writing your request card, simply put it in a larger envelope, seal it and hand it over to your angel. Then let it go.

You may like to put your envelope containing your request card, inside a nice spiritual book on your angel altar, or under an angel statue or picture of an angel, or even an ascended master or saint or beside a crystal or a plant. It is entirely up to you; just do what works best for you at the time.

11) Finally I always say to people "Please give your angels a chance to work on your behalf." Try not to open your request card for at least seven months. People sometimes say to me "Oh I forgot something!" Well that's fine; just write another card out stating your new request.

12) If you ever feel that you wrote a request out that you don't now really want and you have sealed your request card, then simply explain this to your angel and start again.

You can bless the original card and gently shred, tear or burn it. Be thankful that it has brought you this far, making you aware of what you truly want in your life.

13) Do remember that angels only work for your highest good and the highest good of everyone around you. Your angels can never ever work on behalf of a negative or damaging request. That request will simply not be entertained or given any airplay

by the angels, as the heavenly angels only respond to love and goodness.

14) When you have finished writing out your request card, put it away, thanking your Guardian Angel for working with you. Blow out your candle or candles and then simply go about your day.

Altar requests:

Altar requests can simply be written on a small piece of paper and placed on your altar. I like to have a small bowl on my altar for my requests and I often pour a drop of jasmine or rose oil over them as an extra blessing. I then light my candle to bring in the divine love and light of God our Creator.

Always remember, after you have placed your request on your altar just hand it over to your angel, blow out your candle and trust.

It is important to remember that the request or prayer spoken or written from the heart in a loving, positive way shoots directly up to the heavenly realms where the angels can answer. But then it is our loving actions, thoughts, and intentions that seal the deal.

Signs that your Guardian Angel is working with you

When our Guardian Angel is working with us, we can often get a sense of a loving presence, though at certain times our angel can leave us a more obvious sign. These can often be the following symbols:

Feather

1) Your Guardian Angel may drop a small white feather, it's a bit like your angel's symbol, saying "here I am and I'm working with you." One lady told me that just before her request comes about, she often finds a small white feather. Our angels can leave the feather symbol in the most unusual of places; I once found a pure white feather in my shoe, which I took as a sign that I was going in the right direction in my life.

Often in difficult times you may find a small white feather; it's as if your angel is sending you a sign of comfort and support by saying "Here I am; don't worry, things are getting better and I am helping you."

White light

2) When people first start to work with their Guardian Angel, they can often get a sense of white or bright light around them or even beside them. A client once told me that when she was in despair, she called in her angel and she instantly saw a pure white ray of light shining through her window. It seemed to gently float up to where she was sitting and enfolded her with love, warmth and light. Afterwards, she slept peacefully and woke up feeling wonderful.

Orbs

3) More and more people are seeing orbs of light. Orbs are really the angel's presence or energy vibration, that they leave behind when they appear or move (remember angels can move at the speed of light). Orbs can often be round, small, or very large bright white circles of light. Orbs seem to gently glow and are lightly transparent and can often be seen in digital photos.

Angelic Mist

4) In our photos, we can sometimes see angelic mist; this simply is: a beautiful gentle mist, of pure white light, that seems to surround us. I personally feel that this is our angel, placing its magnificent angelic wings of comfort around us for support.

During angel workshops, people can sometimes get a sense of this angelic light or mist, tingling softly around them. Just know that your Guardian Angel has enfolded you in its wings of support. (I feel, as our heavenly angels slow down, the vibration of their wings is like a soft light breeze).

Flowers, Perfume, Scent

5) Sometimes when angels are near, we can get a scent of perfume or flowers. I remember one particular day after meditating to my Guardian Angel, I got an incredible scent of roses. It was as if I was standing in a beautiful garden, with roses all around me. It was quite unusual, as I had been sitting meditating quietly on a busy bus. At first I thought someone had gotten onto the bus with a huge bouquet of flowers; then I realised it was my Guardian Angel's presence.

Music

6) Our angels can often work with us through the vibration of music, as music can indeed lift the soul, helping us to feel more positive. I remember feeling very confused about a house move and I asked my angel to give me a sign that I was doing the right thing by moving. After a while I felt inspired to turn the radio on; a song about angels was playing, so I knew, I was on the right track in moving house and I just trusted in my angel.

Angel gifts or presents

7) An important sign that your Guardian Angel is with you, can be if you receive a present or a card from someone with an angel on it. So many times people tell me of angel presents and cards that they receive out of the blue.

A wonderful story I heard, was from an elderly lady whose husband had recently died. This lady was sitting in a café shortly after her husband's death, feeling very sad and lonely. One of the waitresses in the cafe came up to this elderly lady, smiled and said "I found this angel brooch pin and I thought you might like it".

The waitress had strawberry blonde curly hair and vivid clear green eyes. Later on the elderly lady tried to find the waitress to thank her, as it had been busy in the café earlier. She was told politely by the manager on duty at the time, that no waitress of that description had ever worked there. I really feel very strongly that it was definitely an angel in disguise who gave this lady the angel brooch to help ease the sadness of her husband's passing.

Birds

8) I have found at times, when I am thinking of my Guardian Angel or Archangels, a dove may fly by me or a flock of birds. I feel angels are messengers and often send birds as a sign that they are near. As a child, I always saw a robin when I was out in nature and I still do to this day, for me robins are joyous birds.

I also remember the day before we got married, we got into a taxi to take us to the hotel and just across the road from us, lots of small birds gathered on the roof of our neighbours house; swallows, little finches and robins, they were just singing away. It was truly beautiful, never have I seen so many little birds together. It was as if they were serenading us, on our way to the wedding, with the angels standing beside them.

Guardian Angel Visualisation
(To connect with your Angel)

This is a simple visualisation that anyone can do, as when we start to visualise, we still the mind and connect to our angels and God our creator. The only difference between visualisation and meditation is that visualisation is often longer and can take us on a deeper, more visual spiritual journey. The most important thing however is to enjoy yourself and not to try to hard, or be overly serious. Simply go with the flow, letting your loving Guardian Angel work alongside you.

You may want to read this visualisation several times before you do it. You can read it to yourself or you may like to get someone else to read it aloud to you.

1) First of all make sure your space is tidy. If working with your angel altar, light the candles on your altar and place your requests (if you have any).

2) You may like to play some soft music in the background as this creates a nice ambience, it helps us unwind and mentally prepare. Turn off your mobile phone and close the door.

3) Find a comfortable chair to sit down, where you can put your feet firmly on the ground (sitting is best). If you prefer to lie down, make sure that you have a sturdy matt or bed with a pillow or head rest (to support your head). The most important thing is to be comfortable and feel good.

If you are lying down, try not to fall asleep, as it is always best to meditate or visualise when you are fresh and alert.

4) As you sit or lie down, just breathe gently in your own time (you may like now to do the "white light candle meditation" in chapter three or just continue on).

5) Keep your feet firmly on the ground and then imagine tiny little flowers or roots coming down from the soles of your feet, pushing gently through the floor, spreading out into the ground outside. So your feet feel grounded and safe.

6) Close your eyes gently and visualise a lovely white light, a ray of heavenly white light starting to pour in through the window.

See this beautiful white divine light pouring down on you from the top of your head, to the bottom of your feet.

7) Imagine this beautiful divine white light very softly starting to pour down your forehead, then gliding over your eyelids and gently down your nose, cheeks, mouth and chin.

8) See yourself now pouring this divine white light, softly down your neck and into your shoulders; then pour the light down your arms and into your hands. Your hands become illuminated in this white light.

9) Now visualise this divine white light, pouring gently over your chest area and lovingly down your stomach, your lower body and down your legs to the soles of your feet. Imagine your feet surrounded in this lovely soft, white light (like soft light filled slippers).

10) Let this white divine white light continue to pour down the back of your neck, pouring softly down your back, over your hips and down your calves to your ankles and feet.

11) Your whole body is now surrounded in this white divine light.

12) Gently breathe in this white and light let it fill your mind, body and senses. Feel your mind becoming very wise and calm, you may now like to say the word "peace" or "calm" to yourself.

13) See this beautiful white light, filling up every cell in your body with love and goodness; you now feel very relaxed.

14) Let this divine white light fill up the room; see the room becoming brighter and brighter, full of white light.

15) When you are ready, you may like to call in your Guardian Angel. You could say "Beloved Guardian Angel, step into the room and work with me today", or you can simply say your own invocation.

16) As you call in your Guardian Angel, a really bright white light enters the room, filling you with a sense of complete love and peace; you may get the scent of flowers or perfume or a feeling of unconditional love.

17) When you feel ready, ask your Guardian Angel to work with you: "My beloved angel, I ask that..................." (State your request or wishes).

18) You may get a sense of your Guardian Angel listening calmly to you, even writing your request or wish down, know your request will be delivered instantly to heaven.

19) Let your Guardian Angel, now shower you with divine white light, gently folding its wings around you. Feel the soft downy feathers surrounding you, as you relax back into your angels arms; know that you are truly loved and safe in the embrace of your angel.

20) You may also like to connect with your angel by asking your Guardian Angel its name; simply ask or say: "My Guardian Angel what is your name?" Or "My blessed Guardian Angel what are you called?"

Then see if anything comes to you; a name or an initial may pop into your head, or you might get a feeling of your Angel's name (A lady I know, told me her angel simply wrote its name out for her in her mind; it was "Daniel").

Everyone works and connects with their angel differently, according to their own connection and beliefs. Remember there is no right or wrong way, as your individual connection to your angel is special, just like your fingerprint is unique.

If you do not get a name at first, do not worry, as it will come eventually when the time is right. Do not stress, strain or demand, as working with your angel should be effortless, fun, and enjoyable. Angels do not respond to angry demands or stress; your Guardian Angel will only respond to genuine requests for help.

21) When you are finished talking to your angel, it is important to thank your angel for working with you today, you can simply say: "Thank you, for all your help today."

22) Now say goodbye and see you relaxed and surrounded in this lovely white light. As your Guardian Angel leaves the room, a shower of tiny white feathers fall softly over you. Let these feathers float over you; they are a symbol that your angel is always at your side.

23) Start to visualise the little flowers or roots coming back up through the floor and into the soles of your feet; your feet feel grounded and secure on the floor.

24) Then when you are ready, get up slowly, blow out the candles, and go about your day or evening knowing that your Guardian Angel is always by your side.

Guardian Angel Story

I have always felt very connected to my Guardian Angel, in fact my earliest memory of my angel was when I was about three or four years of age.

I remember quite clearly one day being in the garden and seeing tiny coloured lights, darting around me. Being a toddler, I tried very hard to chase them (I now realise that these lights were fairies, as fairies are the angels of nature). I also remember seeing a slightly bigger light as white as snow. It was like a tennis ball of white light that seemed to follow me for a while. I felt very happy and comforted, as I kept trying to hold this white light in my tiny hand (Sometimes young children, babies and even animals have a very clear connection to their angel, as they are unconditionally loving and pure in spirit, living very much in the present moment).

My next memory, was when I was about six or seven years of age. I remember not being able to sleep and as I looked over at my twin sister who was fast asleep, I felt very restless. I just kept tossing and turning. After a while, I noticed some very small bright lights glowing and swirling around my bedroom ceiling. At first I thought I was dreaming, but it was so beautiful. These lovely white lights were mixed with soft pinks and blues and were truly memorising. A faint sound of music seemed to accompany these lights; it sounded so beautiful, like a choir of truly joyous distant voices singing. As the lights swirled around the ceiling, I remember feeling very happy, and then a gentle voice seemed to tell me that it was okay, I could go to sleep now. I then fell asleep very easily and I slept and slept. To this day, I have never really had any problems getting to sleep.

Looking back, I remember that up until my early teens, I had felt very connected to my Guardian Angel. However, after that time my connection seemed to lesson, it was probably due to peer pressure at school and the influence of others at that time. It then took me many years to reconnect with my angel. It wasn't until I was twenty seven, ill and burnt out, that my angel literally took control of my life and helped me back on track (thank you angels).

As I have said before, our Guardian Angel cannot interfere in our lives, if we do not want them to; this is according to the law of free will. However the reality for me was that my soul subconsciously cried out for help and my Guardian Angel answered the call. I now realise, that my angel had decided, that divine intervention was necessary, to help me start to get my life back on track.

This is indeed what happened to me, at the time a work colleague was quite worried about me and my health, which wasn't great. I had also spent the last couple of years in a very draining relationship that I was trying to find the courage to leave. My colleague then convinced me to make an appointment to see a well known spiritual healer in Dublin called Teresa. Somewhat reluctant and a bit sceptical, I made the appointment to visit this healer.

During my appointment with Teresa, I had a very profound healing and I connected back again with my Guardian Angel. This experience was to change my life forever. Teresa gave me a very gentle aromatherapy massage and did some hands on healing on me. I remember after a few minutes of this healing,

I started to feel very well and happy. As warm heat surrounded me from Teresa's hands and a bright light seemed to pour in through the little window of the therapy room, shining directly down on me, leaving my body feeling warm and nice.

A feeling of pure unconditional love washed over me, it was totally joyous, never had I felt so happy and loved. I felt ecstatic, as if I was floating in a sea of divine love and peace. It was as if my Guardian Angel had put a blanket of divine protective healing light around me. I felt very clear, positive and free, as if the negative veil of illusion that was keeping me from my angel, had been promptly lifted.

After this healing experience my life started to change rapidly. I felt very well and strong, so I decided to leave the negative relationship I was in. I truly felt good in myself and I started to work with my angels, creating and manifesting the life that I had always wanted.

The more I worked alongside my angels, the more my life changed for the better. Little miracles began to flood in for me and I now realised that my Guardian Angel had never left me. I had in fact been the one who had left my angel, so it was wonderful now to awaken fully again to this heavenly goodness. Each day became a miraculous blessing for me.

However, later on in my life, I had to face many changes after the initial euphoria of my spiritual awakening subsided. I found at times that this was hard, even upsetting, to face the many challenges that were sent to me. It was difficult, to let go of the old and embrace the new, but as I walked forward on my newfound path with my Guardian Angel at my side, it seemed to get easier and easier. As my Divine Life Purpose emerged, my soul began to feel happy and free. So now I say a very big "Thank you" to all of my angels.

Chapter 5

Archangels

Archangels: are wise powerful golden light filled angels that have their very own abilities and gifts, often radiating out, various different coloured frequencies of light.

Description: Archangels are quite tall and have very golden auras; they are the guides of our Guardian Angels.

Aura: very bright and golden, radiating powerful loving light and energy.

Colours: gold strong yellow and amber.

Symbol: golden feather, golden ray of light, the sun.

Animal: golden eagle, lion, Pegasus.

Crystals: golden citrine and amber.

Golden Citrine: is an energiser and cleanser. It is a warm, regenerating and creative crystal. Citrine can also be found as a geode (small rock cave formation) or as a bed cluster (small amounts of citrine crystal points on top of a bed of rock). It can be in long crystal point form too (small to large pieces of crystal with a point formation on the end of it).

Amber: is one of the wise crystals, being very grounding and protective. It also revitalises and cleanses and is great for the emotions, mind, body and spirit. Amber is also said to connect you to the ancestors and past lives and can be found in large or small pieces. It is made from tree resin or sap which has become fossilised, so amber is light in weight, golden to clear yellow in colour.

Flower Essence: Oak: is the flower essence that works best with the Archangels, as like the oak tree the Archangels are very wise and help us stay strong. Oak is good for wisdom, helping one also stay strong and determined especially when tired, sick, or faced with difficult times or decisions. Oak can often hold a person up emotionally, helping them persevere, no matter what the circumstances.

Working Together: The Archangels will work with us at any time or place, they have been called the overseeing angels that light our way and each Archangel has its own, specific role or traits. The four main Archangels that most people seem to know are Archangel Michael, Archangel Gabriel, Archangel Raphael and Archangel Uriel (Although there are many more).

Archangels

Archangels can work with us whenever we need help and support, they can also give our Guardian Angel an overview of any situation that we are asking about. Even showing our Guardian Angel what is the best route for us to take. Archangels are wise, protective, creative and loving; they also have a direct line to heaven.

When an Archangel enters the room, you can almost sense it, as a very bright light seems to radiate and glow around the room. You may also feel warm and happy, supported and cared for. It's as if a loving wise presence is there lighting our way, therefore Archangels truly are the older angelic brothers and sisters of our Guardian Angels.

When I work with the presence of the Archangels, I always get a great sense of peace, as if a bridge to heaven has been created for me to ask for my requests or prayers. Archangels, like our Guardian Angels love to help us; again we just have to reach out and ask the Archangels. Then they will become our spiritual guides and teachers here on the earth.

In this chapter, we will work with the seven main Archangels, Archangel Michael, Archangel Raphael, Archangel Gabriel, Archangel Uriel, Archangel Jophiel, Archangel Zadkiel, and Arch- angel Haniel. We will be looking at the Archangels and their individual roles and traits, and we will also ask the Archangels to bring peace, harmony and happiness into our lives.

Affirmations and prayers to the Archangels.

"Mighty Archangels be with me now."

"Archangels surround me in your golden healing light or wings."

"Archangels of the heavenly realms, I ask you to work with me now, help me with the following situation ...."(Describe the situation, you would like help with).

"Golden Archangels shine your ray of light around me or... (name the person) now."

(Thank you, Amen).

This Archangel meditation is easy and effective to do, especially if you need support or even a boost of energy.

Or, if you would just like to simply de-stress and feel more positive. When the Archangels work together as a group they are supremely powerful and supportive.

Archangel Golden Light Meditation

1) First of all, find a quiet place to meditate or be in the peace, sit in a comfortable chair or even in a nice room or out in the garden.

2) Then visualise little flowers or roots coming down from the soles of your feet, pushing through the ground and spreading out into the soil, really grounding you to the earth.

3) Breathe in very gently through your nose, exhaling from your mouth, do this three times, then feel yourself start to unwind.

4) Visualise your body relaxing and feel at peace.

5) When you are ready you can ask the Archangels to come into the room, you can say "Archangels work with me now" or "Golden Archangels be with me."

6) Then imagine a golden ray of light coming into the room, see this light shinning over the top of your head, gently pouring over you.

7) Let this light, fall very gently down your head, face, neck, gliding down your body, from the top of your head to the bottom of your feet.

8) Now visualise your body completely relaxing as this golden light pours down over you. It's a bit like a blanket of golden light surrounding you.

9) Breathe in this golden light, let it fill your mind and body; feel completely illuminated in this golden light.

10) See the golden light, dissolving all worries, fears, stress and negativity from your mind and body.

11) Let go of all worries now and just go with the flow. Imagine this light pouring inside your body and see it filling up your cells

with this gentle golden relaxing light. Let your cells become relaxed, rejuvenated, energised and positive, feel good and happy.

12) You might like to say the following affirmation: "My body is now full of loving energy and well-being."

13) Now see yourself getting stronger, full of energy and positivity.

14) Visualise the little flowers or roots, coming up from the ground and going back into the soles of your feet, feel grounded and strong.

15) Sense yourself back in the chair, your upper and lower body present in the chair, your head and neck very relaxed and present on your shoulders. When you are ready count from one to seven; then very gently open your eyes, flex your muscles and get up, or if you feel like a lie down go to bed.

16) Just know the golden Archangels are with you now.

Archangel Story

As far as I can remember, I have always had a fascination with the different Archangels, as during certain difficult times in my life they have always surrounded and helped me.

I remember very clearly one day as a teenager, walking home from secondary school. It was a lovely sunny day and I knew that our summer holidays were fast approaching. I felt happy, as I hummed a song gently to myself and started to walk the long road up to our house. Within a few minutes of walking up the road, I had a strange feeling, as my stomach started to flutter and my heart began beating fast. My hands felt clammy and my legs were heavy like lead, what was happening to me I wondered as I continued walking up the road, the reality hit me and I froze, I saw the school bully from my class with her army of followers walking towards me.

I now realise that my Guardian Angel, was trying to alert me by sending me varying messages through my body, but it was too late, as there was simply no-where to turn off the road and it was a straight road up to our house where we lived.

I suddenly began to feel faint, breathing rapidly, desperately trying to steady myself, not knowing how I would pass by this sneering entourage of school girls. Then suddenly out of the blue, something simply wonderful happened, that still to this day makes me smile.

Within a few minutes, everything around me started to slow down, it's as if I were in a beautiful dream, a golden haze or mist just seem to cover me, a bit like a protective gentle shield. I then got a sense of several very tall beings almost like guards, standing around me in a circle with their backs to me, holding golden staffs (I now know that these beings were the Archangels).

With the Archangels beside me, my feet seemed to glide effortlessly up the road. I felt very confident and tall, as the bully and her gang approached, they seemed to me at the time to be very small indeed; in fact I didn't even notice them. When they passed me by on the road, they were making rude faces at me, but it just didn't seem to bother me at all. I simply looked straight ahead and walked up the road.

Looking back, it's as if everything was being blocked out on purpose, the sounds and faces around me seemed muffled, as I glided effortlessly along with the Archangels in my golden circle of protection and love. I felt blissfully unaware of everything, as if I were being completely removed from the situation. I really didn't have a care in the world, I was feeling great, as if nothing could undermine or affect me

As the afternoon progressed, I started to remember what had happened and yet even then it didn't seem real, almost as if I had been viewing myself on a projector screen. However deep inside of me, I knew it had all been very real and I smiled as I recalled the look of anger and disbelief on the bully's face when I hadn't flinched at the name calling. I knew then that she had felt disempowered and powerless, as I had just ignored her; she was totally surprised at my reaction, even a bit envious.

Shortly after my experience with the Archangels, I was able to detach easily from the bullies at school and their antics. I felt that I had truly regained my inner power and strength and I knew that things could only improve now; and they slowly did.

It's important to remember that the Archangels can indeed join together as a group to guide and support you. They can also intervene for the highest good of everyone involved (as the Archangels, are your direct line to Heaven) often forming a spiritual bridge that can bring miracles to the earth. In my case they formed a shield of golden light around me as a teenager, to help me move forward in my life, so I could feel back in my power and get on with my life again. So a big thank you, Archangels.

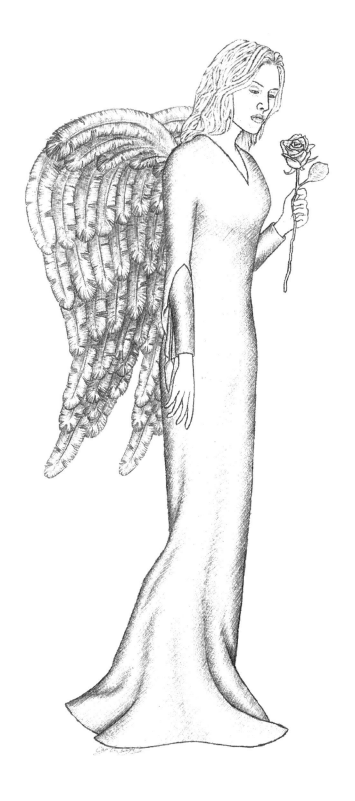

Chapter 6

Archangel Haniel

Archangel Haniel: is one of the angels of love and is said to be connected to the angels of virtue. Archangel Haniel has loving, gentle, yin energy and is known to be female. I see Archangel Haniel as a beautiful, loving, graceful, compassionate Archangel, who can help you love yourself and others, often guiding you towards finding true love.

Description: Archangel Haniel radiates a golden aura often mixed with rose pink light and wears a pink gown of light. Archangel Haniel can be seen carrying a pale pink rose, a symbol of new beginnings in our love life.

Aura: very bright, golden rose pink, radiating love and light.

Colours: gold and Rose pink.

Symbol: pink feather, rose, Venus, love heart, pink orb, or mist.

Animal: swan, unicorn, honey bee, deer.

Crystal: rose quartz and rhodochrosite.

Rose Quartz: is a beautiful rose pink crystal, very much associated with love. It is the crystal or stone of pure unconditional love, bringing self love and peace. Rose quartz is normally a light rose to dark pink in colour and is one of the crystals that works very well with clear quartz and amethyst. It can be obtained in raw (or rough) form, or tumbled (polished). Rose quartz can also be in point form, or as a crystal bed. A very popular crystal, rose quartz can be fashioned into heart shaped stones, candle holders, oil burners, bookends and jewellery. A rose quartz pendant or necklace worn close to the heart is said to bring true love, healing and compassion into your life.

Rhodochrosite: is a wonderful deep pink crystal or stone. It has soft white markings on it and is called the divine soul-mate crystal as it represents selfless, unconditional love. Rhodochrosite is said to heal a broken heart, and can help if you have endured a difficult relationship. It is mainly obtained in raw or polished form and is very popular worn as a pendant or necklace.

Many people have told me that working with rose quartz and rhodochrosite crystals have helped enhance their love life, helping them to feel more positive towards love and new relationships (In my own case, I was wearing a rhodochrosite pendant, when I first met my husband to be).

Flower Essence: *wild rose:* Is good for self love, nurturing, harmony and for developing your talents. It's considered a very loving happy essence.

Working Together: Archangel Haniel really is a wonderful, loving, healing Archangel that can help us understand how to love ourselves and others. We can invoke Archangel Haniel at any time and she will shower us with pink loving light. Archangel Haniel can help us move towards meeting our true life partner and will even open the door by lighting our way and showing us how to proceed forward.

Working with Archangel Haniel

When I work with Archangel Haniel, I instantly feel very calm and positive. Archangel Haniel can help us to love ourselves and others unconditionally, so that we can move forward positively in all of our relationships.

Very often I find when I work with clients and Archangel Haniel, the results can often be very impressive. As the invisible hurts and fears that have been stored away in our hearts can often be slowly released. Archangel Haniel's unconditional love and support can set us free from emotional pain and fear, helping us move forward towards creating healthy relationships.

Sometimes people are only used to giving love and are not able to receive love for themselves. However to keep your heart, mind and physical self healthy and in balance it is important to give but also to receive love. If we only ever give love, we may start to create an imbalance in our relationships, attracting selfish partners or friends (energy vampires) who are disrespectful of our needs and can very easily drain us of energy. This may even cause a deep resentment within us, emotionally and physically. So it is very important to remember that love, like life, should be an effortless balance of giving and receiving.

There are however, different times in our lives, when we are simply meant to give pure unconditional love. For example: as in the case of one person in a relationship supporting another through a difficult time. Or a mother looking after and nurturing a sick child or working with the elderly and so forth. Unconditional love is very important in life and in the community, as giving lovingly from the heart connects us directly to our true divine spirit.

However, unconditional love only becomes an issue when someone is constantly taking advantage of you and playing on your good nature. They can even be very aware that they are doing this, as it can make them feel strong and powerful. But this is taking and not giving. These people can be very demanding, manipulative and constant high maintenance.

This can sometimes happen in a romantic relationship, friendships or indeed in families. It can be a tough learning curve, but you can always ask Archangel Haniel and the angels of love to help you face this issue. So there is more of a balance in all your relationships.

Again in families, all love should be unconditional. I have found, that some people, who have often been brought up in a demanding family dynamic, where love is conditional, can often feel very lonely and truly crave their Divine Soul-Mate (I always say, that just because they are your family, does not mean that they are your "soul family"). Often our soul can chose a difficult family situation, to learn from, so that we can grow and move forward and become better people.

Remember, there will always be some family or even friends, that you will get on with and others that you won't. This is life, but you should never put up with bad behaviour or conditional love or bullying, because it's expected of you in the family or indeed in friendships or relationships.

Often when we start to put value on ourselves, by learning to heal and love ourselves again. We begin to walk the path of freedom, sometimes even connecting and attracting our true love or Divine Soul-Mate along the way.

It is natural and normal to want to meet your Divine Soul-Mate and life Partner, but it should happen in divine timing and never in a forced or desperate fashion.

When people first start working with Archangel Haniel and the angels of love, they can often get a sense of a soft pink light around them, accompanied by the scent of roses. They may even start to feel a little more open, optimistic and positive, towards their relationships and love life.

This is a wonderful meditation, to help you feel loved and supported. Archangel Haniel can help soothe away any worries or anxieties. I find this meditation of great comfort when I am having a bit of "me" time (which we all need).

Archangel Haniel Pink Light Meditation (For comfort and support)

1) First of all find a quiet place to relax in.

2) You might like to light a pink candle, freshen up the room with rose spray or oil, or even have a piece of rose quartz crystal beside you.

3) Then either sit or lie down, always making sure you are comfortable.

4) Play some gentle music or just work with the silence.

5) Breathe gently in and out in your own time and space, feel the peace in the room and become one with the stillness.

6) Get a sense of your feet and imagine tiny rose buds coming down from the soles of your feet anchoring you into the ground, so your feet feel grounded and secure.

7) Ask Archangel Haniel to step into the room.

8) You might like to say: "Archangel Haniel, I call upon you (here today) to work with me now. Thank you, Amen."

9) Visualise a pink light pouring into the room and get a sense of Archangel Haniel's presence. See Archangel Haniel, in a flowing pink gown with a pink light all around her, or just imagine a loving pink mist or light gently floating into the room where you are.

10) Feel the pure unconditional love all around you. It's as if Archangel Haniel has just put her beautiful wings of comfort and support around you. Relax back in this loving presence.

11) Sense Archangel Haniel, pouring her pink loving light over you, a bit like a shower of pink light pouring directly over you, from the top of your head, to the bottom of your feet.

12) Let this wonderful loving pink light pour over you now and feel good.

13) Breathe in this light, let it fill your mind and body, with unconditional love and peace.

14) Hand any worries you have over to Archangel Haniel, especially if you need guidance about a relationship or you just need support. Let Archangel Haniel take care of everything now. Then thank Archangel Haniel, let go and relax.

15) Visualise the little rose bud flowers coming out of the ground back into the soles of your feet, your feet feel relaxed and comfortable.

16) Breathe gently in your own time and space, move your body and get up when you are ready. Blow out any candles. Trust that Archangel Haniel is working with you now.

Affirmations to Archangel Haniel:

"Archangel Haniel, help me love and nurture myself today."

"Archangel Haniel, send me love and light and guide my way."

"Archangel Haniel, open the way for my true love and Divine Soul-Mate, to come into my life."

"Archangel Haniel, let unconditional love come into my life today."

(Thank you.)

To write or call upon Archangel Haniel and the angels of love you can say:

"Archangel Haniel, work with me today and help me open my heart to love. I call upon you to help me meet my true divine soul mate. Let this (man or woman) be kind, loving, etc": then list the qualities you desire.

(Remember to always ask for the spiritual qualities in your relationship, but do go for gold and really list what you desire in a positive loving way, and remember to have fun too).

Your true love will always be sent to you, if it is for your highest good. But sometimes you may have to wait a little bit longer, as events happen when they are ready, in Divine Timing (God's timing). However, the angels will always improve your love life and can even help you feel good too. It's important to have fun, but also to be aware that you may have to do some honest work on yourself.

It is true, that love is indeed our birthright and Archangel Haniel and the angels of love can help us, but in order to meet our true love, our Divine Soul-Mate, we must first become what we seek. Only by truly loving ourselves unconditionally and naturally radiating out this perfect love, only then can we attract our beloved Soul-Mate, our Divine life partner.

It is important to remember, that if the shoe fits wear it. However we cannot simply squeeze our foot into the wrong shoe size, no matter how hard we try, or we will end up with blisters. People often try to do this in relationships and it only creates heartache and pain.

The key is: to be open minded and be willing to learn and trust, whilst working with the angels. Yet do have fun along the way and believe you deserve the best (true unconditional divine love).

The following visualisation with Archangel Haniel can help guide you towards meeting your true love. It can also help you move forward in your relationship or marriage in a more positive and loving way.

Archangel Haniel Visualisation

1) Find a quiet space to work in or if it's a nice day sit in your garden or a somewhere peaceful out in nature.

2) If you are going to work with your angel altar, you can place a pink candle, rose quartz or rhodochrosite crystals (if available) on the altar. As this helps invoke the presence of Archangel Haniel (if you are going to work with candles, it is important to be awake or alert during the visualisation).

3) You can also hold a piece of rose quartz or rhodochrosite in your writing hand.

4) A nice angel spray or room spray can be nice to use or even have rose incense lighting.

5) You can write a Divine soul-mate request or altar request to Archangel Haniel if you wish.

6) You may like to play gentle angelic or classical music while you do this visualisation (I often like to put a soft pink blanket or wrap around my shoulders, to make my self, feel comfortable and supported).

7) Now, you are ready to begin. First of all find a comfortable chair or if you are lying down a mat or bed with a head rest or pillow. Feel yourself starting to relax and switch off your phone. Become aware of the peace, the music, the pink colour of the candle, the crystals, and the sounds of Mother Nature.

8) Keep your feet firmly on the ground and if you are outside and the grass is clean and warm you might like to remove your shoes and socks to connect with the earth. Start to visualise, tiny little rose buds coming down from the soles of your feet, pushing through the floor, grounding and connecting you to Mother Earth.

9) Relax back and get a sense of your body unwinding. All you have to do is become aware of your surroundings and breathe gently in your own time and space. Know you are very safe and this is your time to connect with Archangel Haniel and all the angels of love and relationships.

10) Start to visualise a golden light, a bit like a ray of sun light pouring in through the window. See this light from heaven shinning down on you, from the top of your head to the bottom of your feet.

11) Visualise this golden heavenly light, starting to very gently glide down your forehead, over your eyelids, your cheeks, nose, mouth, chin and neck.

12) Take this golden light and pour it slowly down your shoulders, your arms and into your hands. See your hands now surrounded in this golden light.

13) Pour this golden light slowly over your chest area and gently down your stomach and your lower body. Then right down your legs to the soles of your feet. Visualise your feet surrounded in this golden light.

14) Imagine this lovely warming gentle golden light pouring slowly down the back of your head, down your neck into your shoulder blades. Then pour the light slowly down your back and gently over your hips.

15) Continue to pour this golden light over your hips, down your legs to your ankles and underneath your feet.

16) Your whole body is now surrounded in this golden light, from the top of your head to the bottom of your feet.

17) Visualise this light, getting brighter and brighter around you, so bright, as if you are sitting or lying in a golden circle of divine light.

18) Breathe in this golden light, let it fill your mind, your body, every pore of your being.

19) Sense your mind, becoming wise and calm and visualise every cell in your body being filled with this golden light (You can literally visualise your cells as golden, healthy and well, with little happy smiling faces full of positive energy and light).

20) Let the room fill up with this divine golden light, becoming brighter and brighter.

21) Then either silently or verbally, call in your Guardian Angel; you can simply say: "My Guardian Angel, step into the room now, work with me today."

22) Get a sense of your Guardian Angel, stepping softly into the room, surrounded in a pure white light, your angel, showers you with this white light.

23) Receive all this goodness and light from your angel and ask your angel to be by your side during this visualisation. (If you have a special request now hand it over to your angel).

24) Imagine yourself taking your angel's hand and let your Guardian Angel lead you out of the room.

25) Visualise yourself and your Guardian Angel, walking together out in the countryside. The sun is shinning and the sky is very blue. There is such a feeling of peace, around you; breathe in the blueness of the sky and feel the golden sunlight and the light breeze on your face. There may be trees or wildflowers nearby, you may even see birds or small animals and you feel wonderful, it's like heaven on earth.

26) Continue walking with your angel and let the golden sunlight illuminate your path, forming rays of light all around you. Just follow the light until you come to a gate; you then tell your angel you would like to go through the gate to see where it leads.

27) As you walk through the gate you realise you are in a beautiful garden; the grass is a lovely emerald green colour, there are trees, bushes, flowers. There may even be a water feature or pond or stream present.

28) In the middle of the garden, there is a lovely comfortable pink chair with soft pink cushions; you decide to sit down now on this chair.

29) Breathe in the goodness all around you and relax, you start to get the most beautiful scent of roses and you notice the rose bushes are all around you. Let the colours and smell of the roses just fill your senses.

30) After a while a lovely pink mist just seems to float effortlessly into the garden and you feel very loved and supported.

31) A wonderful feeling of pure unconditional love seems to pour around you. It's as if you have been enfolded in pink loving wings.

32) Your Guardian Angel tells you that Archangel Haniel (the Angel of love) is by your side. As you become more aware of Archangel Haniel, you get a sense of a beautiful female Archangel dressed in rose pink, radiating a pink and golden aura.

33) Connect with Archangel Haniel, if you would like to feel loved and supported ask Archangel Haniel for this now.

34) If you feel you would like to meet your true love, your divine life partner and soul-mate, ask Archangel Haniel to work with you. Even if you want to improve your current relationship or marriage, or if you just want more romance and fun, Archangel Haniel will work with you (all you have to do is ask).

35) See Archangel Haniel, placing her loving wings around you, as you ask for your requests. If you truly want to meet your true love and divine soul mate, then do specify what qualities you desire in the person. Try to be specific and clear. Then when you are ready, simply hold a vision in your mind of the partner and relationship you would like to have.

If you are not sure, what you desire in a partner, just hand your request or prayer over to Archangel Haniel and the angels of love and let them work on your behalf.

36) After you have placed your request with Archangel Haniel, just relax back in Archangel Haniel's loving presence and now trust that all is being taken care of.

37) Let Archangel Haniel shower you now, with pink angelic light, from the top of your head to the bottom of your feet and experience this pure unconditional love. Know that everything

is working out and let this loving healing light nurture and support you.

38) When you are ready, thank Archangel Haniel for all her help. See Archangel Haniel, handing you a beautiful pink rose, a symbol of new beginnings in your love life.

Take your Guardian Angel's hand and say goodbye to Archangel Haniel and the angels of love, knowing that you can always come back here, to this heavenly rose garden and work again with Archangel Haniel.

39) Leave the garden with your Guardian Angel and walk back out through the gate and into the countryside. Let the blue sky, golden sunlight just illuminate your path. Your Guardian Angel, now leads you back into the room or peaceful setting, from where you started.

40) Feel yourself sitting firmly in the chair, or lying on the bed or mat and visualise the little flowers (rose buds) coming up from the ground, back into the soles of your feet; your feet feel very grounded.

41) Get a sense that you are back in the room or peaceful setting and feel your body present in the chair or on the bed. Your neck and shoulders relaxed, arms and hands by your side. Then breathing gently in your own time and space, count from one to seven; then open your eyes.

42) You are now back in the room or out in the peaceful setting. Then slowly get up (stretch if you need to) blow out your candle, rearrange the room if necessary and go about your business in a loving positive way.

Archangel Haniel Story

Many people have told me, that when they meditate or visualise with Archangel Haniel, they automatically get a great sense of peace and comfort around them. A feeling of pure unconditional love starts to surround them and they start to feel more optimistic about love. Sometimes their marriage or relationships even improve, becoming more positive and loving.

A young man, I knew, told me that after working with Archangel Haniel and the angels of love, his love life seemed to improve and he was simply led to his true love.

Archangel Haniel, can also help you love and nurture yourself, especially if you do not feel good about yourself or your love life. Archangel Haniel can help increase your self confidence whilst helping you move forward in a positive loving way. Working with Archangel Haniel can be very comforting indeed, especially in times of despair, as Archangel Haniel, radiates pure, unconditional, divine love. Archangel Haniel can help heal broken hearts and help you fall in love again.

I now include the following true story:

During a very difficult time in my love life, I began to slowly fall into deep despair. My friends at the time, took me out and about, so I could meet a "nice man". Which I did and I was strongly persuaded to go on a date with him a few days later.

Much to my regret, as the nice man was not really that "nice". He had his own issues to sort out, so the date ended up being a disaster. Afterwards, I felt very lonely and isolated, despite cheering up phone calls from my friends. After nearly twelve years of being in three major relationships, I just felt enough was enough.

At the time, I had been working with my angels for about six months or so and I was well aware of how to work with my angels, especially the angels of love. But I was heart broken and I felt that my angels had truly abandoned me. One rainy evening, after watching mindless television, my heart was aching. So I poured myself a glass of wine and I started to cry softly, eventually lying on the floor.

Within a few minutes, I heard a very distinct clear gentle loving voice. It seemed to say, "Get up off the floor now" I hesitantly obeyed, mesmerised at first and I sat back down on the couch. An overwhelming feeling to lie down came over me, so I lay back down slowly on my couch. As I closed my eyes, the most wonderful feeling swept over me; it was as if multitudes of angels had entered the room, radiating pure unconditional love and light. I felt a lovely warm light breeze around me and I saw a pink ball of light that seemed to glow and glow, until it dissolved gently over me, showering me with its lovely pink light.

I felt, as if I were being covered in a pink blanket of divine love. Peace surrounded me and I slept. I awoke late in the afternoon, feeling completely refreshed, alive and joyous, as if all sorrow had been lifted. My heart was no longer heavy. I smiled and thanked the angels for this miracle, as I knew in my heart that Archangel Haniel and the angels of love had been with me all night.

Later on that day, I felt inspired to take a pink piece of card and write to Archangel Haniel and the angels of love. I explained all of my love life to them and I asked them to help me meet my true Divine Soul-Mate. I then proceeded to describe in clear detail, the kind of partner I wanted, listing all of the qualities and attributes. I sealed my request card and handed it over to Archangel Haniel and the angels of love.

I then simply let go of my request and I trusted that the angels would work on my behalf. In truth, the more I let go of my love request, the more I felt completely free and I knew that my right partner was on the way.

Later on that evening, I had a wonderful vision. I got a sense, of a lovely man trying to connect with me in spirit.

I could only barely see his face and I remember he was very kind, patient and unconditionally loving. I saw our souls reaching out, smiling at each other and yet the bond and connection I felt to him, seemed to transcend time and space. It was so beautiful and real, that I knew it was my Divine Soul-Mate looking for me too.

Four years later, when I was truly ready to meet my Divine Soul-Mate (my husband to be) it just happened like a miracle and we both knew it (Thank you angels).

Just one last thing, when I tell this true story of my love life, people often say to me "Well it took four years for you both to meet". Yes this was true for me, but it can also take four minutes.   It just depends if you are ready or not. Back then I wasn't ready as I had to do a bit of healing and inner work on myself, learning to love myself again and starting to feel good.

So I did just that and I had four great years of learning. Yes, there were highs and lows, but I knew all the time that I was moving towards a better outcome, so I just believed and trusted.

When I did eventually meet my husband to be, I was indeed ready (we both were and we knew it). It worked out effortlessly, as it was our time to meet. It was indeed Divine Timing (God's / Universal Timing).

Our relationship was effortless, easy and loving. I truly feel, that Archangel Haniel and all the angels of love came together to help us connect again in this lifetime.

For this I will always be eternally grateful.

Chapter 7

Archangel Raphael

Archangel Raphael: means "Healer of God", Archangel Raphael, is one of the main Archangels, alongside Archangels Michael, Gabriel and Uriel and he has many healing angels, working at his side.

Archangel Raphael is said to be the Archangel that can heal our bodies, minds and spirit. Raphael is also considered to be the patron of those who travel and of those who work in the healing or medical profession. If you ever feel drawn to working in the healing profession then Archangel Raphael is the Archangel to call upon.

Description: Archangel Raphael is said to have a very golden and emerald green aura or presence. Raphael is often seen wearing an emerald green tunic or robe of light. Raphael can be seen also holding a caduceus (a universal, medicinal healing symbol, with two snakes intertwined) staff of light, with a clear quartz or emerald crystal at the top. Archangel Raphael is associated with all the air signs (Gemini, Libra and Aquarius).

Aura: very bright, golden, with emerald green lights.

Colours: gold and emerald

Symbol: emerald green feather, diamond, wooden staff, waterfall, crystal healing wand, basket or horn of plenty (containing various fruit and vegetables) green pastures and valleys.

Animal: frog, fish, snake.

Crystal: clear quartz and emerald.

Clear Quartz: is probably one of the most powerful healing crystals there is. It is normally a very clear white transparent colour and can be found worldwide. Clear quartz can be tumbled or rough and can often be found in crystal clusters or beds. Its most popular use is in crystal point form.

Clear quartz is said, to raise our aura (bio-magnetic energy field around the body) and it is said to boost the immune system. It can often release negative energy stored around the body, absorbing and dissolving it. Working with a clear quartz crystal can automatically energise you and raise your vibration and spirit to the heavenly realms. Clear quartz therefore, is the master healer of crystals and is said to retain its healing knowledge throughout time.

Emerald: is thought to be the stone of inspiration, patience and loyalty. Emeralds are quite expensive when cut as gemstones and are a vibrant green colour. Raw or rough emeralds have a more subdued or cloudy green colour and are cheaper to buy. Emerald is said to be the healing crystal of the heart, balancing all the emotions, as emerald green is a very healing colour on the mind and body and is associated with Mother Nature.

Flower Essence: *Olive:* flower essence is said to be one of the essences of healing. Olive is very good for fatigue, especially if you are recovering from an illness or feeling depleted, as olive can give you a lift, slowly boosting your energy. Essence of olive or even virgin olive oil is said to be very healing. It has long been the secret ingredient and healing elixir of the Mediterranean people, down through the ages.

Working Together: All we have to do is invoke Archangel Raphael; then this mighty Archangel with his healing angels will put his emerald green light around us, showering us with his healing light.

Working with Archangel Raphael

When we work with Archangel Raphael, healing miracles can literally surround us, as Archangel Raphael, is God our Creator's healing messenger from heaven. When we call in or invoke Archangel Raphael, we can receive great peace, healing and comfort.

It's important to remember, that Archangel Raphael will work with you regardless of your background or belief system, as the healing angels are there for everyone. A wonderful elderly man, I once knew called "Tommy", often said to me, "I don't really have a huge connection to the angels, but I do believe in Archangel Raphael and his healing light." When we ask Archangel Raphael to work with us, he often puts his emerald green healing light around us or even around the situation that we are asking about, bringing in healing and balance.

We can also ask Archangel Raphael, to put his emerald cloak of light around anyone we know that is sick, or recovering from illness, be it physical or emotional. Archangel Raphael is known to be one of the angels of peace and healing. People who believe in the power of Mother Mary (Christ's mother on Earth) have often seen a beautiful healing Archangel accompanying her to the various locations, helping with petitions and requests for healing.

Archangel Raphael's healing presence is indeed very powerful. Yet Archangel Raphael often works with us in a very subtle way, never interfering, but by gently healing and inspiring us, giving us the healing knowledge that we seek. Archangel Raphael is the ultimate Angelic healer of the physical body, but he can also help us let go of emotionally negative or even upsetting thought patterns.

There are times that we do not heal for various reasons as we may not be ready to let go of the illness. We may even have more to learn from it, or simply it might not be for our highest good in this moment to heal. Nevertheless, we can still work with Archangel Raphael and all his healing angels, asking to improve our health, and help us to remain positive and optimistic. Archangel Raphael can also help alleviate pain and suffering, so we can manage, giving us the courage to move forward and keep going.

Often people with different physical and emotional conditions, who work with Archangel Raphael tell me that after working with Archangel Raphael they feel supported and at peace. They are also sometimes led to great doctors, healers and holistic practitioners, who can help them. Sometimes our own personal healing journey can enlighten us and others in a similar situation.

There are many people, who have had miraculous healings, whilst working with Archangel Raphael (I myself am amongst them). Archangel Raphael came into my life when I least expected it (no doubt through the prayers of family and friends) putting me in the path of the right healer. Archangel Raphael, guided by God Our Creator, literally helped me heal emotionally overnight, while I improved physically over the next couple of months. For my "healing miracle", I will always be eternally grateful to Archangel Raphael and the healing angels.

Archangel Raphael, is also said to be the patron of animals, therefore if you have any animals that need healing, you can ask Archangel Raphael to work with them. Archangel Raphael is considered to be one of the angels of nature, so you can ask Archangel Raphael to work with you in your garden and help improve your gardening skills.

It is said, in many scriptures and holy books, that Archangel Raphael can help you travel freely and easily to where ever you have to go, keeping your spirits high along the journey. So you can call upon Archangel Raphael, to help you if you are travelling or going on long journeys. Many of my clients have told me that when doing their driving test, they called in Archangel Raphael and instantly felt a wonderful presence beside them.

I petitioned Archangel Raphael when my husband and I needed a new car and it came in a truly wonderful way for us.

Ways to work with Archangel Raphael

You can ask Archangel Raphael:

1) For physical, emotional and spiritual healing.

2) To help you travel safely (showing you the right way).

3) To help you find the right doctor, healer, holistic practitioner.

4) For financial abundance especially for the home, a new car or to do a healing, holistic or medical course or degree.

5) To heal and look after all animals.

6) To help improve your garden and connect you to Mother Nature.

7) For inner peace and tranquillity.

8) If you are tired and lack energy or feel sluggish, you can ask Archangel Raphael to boost your energy levels, so you can feel optimistic about life again.

9) If you really need a break, you can ask Archangel Raphael to help you find the time and money to have a wonderful holiday.

10) When you need to buy or rent a new home, you can ask Archangel Raphael to show you or guide you to the right location.

Archangel Raphael, is also said also to work with food therefore, it is a good idea to call upon Archangel Raphael to bless your food. Blessing our food with love and gratitude can raise the energy vibration of our meal, making it taste better, digest easier and boost the vitamin and mineral content in the food which can help us. Archangel Raphael can help us eat healthily and exercise regularly too.

Archangel Raphael is said to have multitudes of healing angels by his side, assisting him in his healing work. I have often seen Archangel Raphael working alongside Archangel Michael (the protector), even assisting Archangel Michael, if any healing is needed from any physical or emotional situations.

If you ever have experienced any kind of physical or psychic attack or fright, first call in Archangel Michael to protect you, then afterwards call in Archangel Raphael for healing. Raphael will surround you with his emerald green healing light. Both Archangels work very well together in perfect balance, as Archangel Michael has a very strong protective, yet loving yang presence and Archangel Raphael, has a gentle, loving, yin, strong healing presence. Remember with both of these Archangels at your side, things can only improve.

Archangel Raphael is also said to work with all the earthly healers, through their hands, often helping miraculous healings to occur. Raphael is known as the Archangel that can enlighten many doctors and scientists, helping directly impart healing knowledge from God our Creator towards pioneering new and positive medical and holistic treatments. When working with Archangel Raphael, it can be useful to have Raphael's healing crystals to hand: clear quartz or emerald.

The following meditation can help you to connect with Archangel Raphael, if you need any physical or emotional healing. You can also ask Archangel Raphael for healing on behalf of someone else.

Meditation with Archangel Raphael (Emerald Green Healing Light)

1) Find a nice space to relax in and either sit or lie down (make sure your head is always supported).

2) Light a candle if possible.

3) Take three gentle breaths, inhale and exhale with each breath you take, start to relax.

4) Imagine or visualise tiny little flowers or roots coming down from the soles of your feet, pushing into the ground and spreading out downward into the soil, connecting you to Mother Nature. Your feet feel safe and grounded.

5) Relax back, call in Archangel Raphael, you can say "Archangel Raphael be with me now."

6) Get a sense of a soft emerald green light coming into the room. Archangel Raphael emerges from this light wearing emerald green robes of light and carrying a caduceus healing staff.

7) Archangel Raphael's aura is emerald green and golden; and he radiates this light all around him.

8) Breathe in this beautiful emerald green and golden light. Let it fill your mind, body and spirit; feel this goodness.

9) If you need any physical healing or emotional support, just ask Archangel Raphael to work with you now. You might like to say: "Archangel Raphael work with me today; send me healing for...." (explain your physical or emotional condition).

If you are asking for healing on behalf of someone else, or for a situation that needs healing, simply explain this to Archangel Raphael.

10) Visualise Archangel Raphael placing his emerald green light around you, or the person or situation that needs healing.

11) Simply breathe in and absorb this beautiful emerald green healing light and let it fill every cell in your body helping you get better (or see this emerald green healing light, now covering the person or situation you are asking about).

12) Keeping it effortless, continue to breathe in this healing light, while gently relaxing back in Archangel Raphael's loving embrace. Feel the comfort, support and peace that engulfs you.

13) When you are ready, thank Archangel Raphael, and know that Raphael and all the healing angels are with you now.

14) Sense yourself back in the space, either sitting or lying down. Visualise the little flowers or roots coming slowly back up from the ground, back into your feet; your feet now feel very grounded and secure.

15) Slowly flex your lower then upper body and stretch out if you need to. Then get up, blow out the candle, and go about your day knowing Archangel Raphael is by your side.

Affirmations and prayers to Archangel Raphael:

"Archangel Raphael, be with me now."

"Blessed Archangel Raphael, work with me today."

"Archangel Raphael, let me heal from ....."(describe your ailment).

"Archangel Raphael, put your emerald green healing light around me."

"Archangel Raphael, shine your emerald green healing light on..." (describe your condition, or the person's).

"Archangel Raphael, help me eat sensibly and healthily and enjoy doing exercise."

"Archangel Raphael, bring peace and healing to...." (describe the situation).

"Archangel Raphael, assist me in all my healing work and pour your healing light through my hands."

"Archangel Raphael, open the way for a wonderful holiday to come my way."

"Archangel Raphael, send me the right bus or train or plane that I need."

"Archangel Raphael, be with me now as I travel and let me be on time."

"Open the way Archangel Raphael, for financial abundance to come my way, to pay for my holistic or medical courses."

"Archangel Raphael, send me financial assistance for my home (describe what you need) or a new car (again describe what you want)."

"Archangel Raphael, heal my pet (describe)."

"Archangel Raphael, work with me in my garden and let it flourish now."

Remember: Thank Archangel Raphael, then just believe, trust and let go.

The following visualisation with Archangel Raphael is for general healing and to help you feel good. Also if you want to change career and move into the healing profession, or if you need abundance or help with your holidays or travelling plans, then this visualisation is for you.

Visualisation with Archangel Raphael

1) First of all find a comfortable space to visualise in (you can lie or sit down, if lying down keep your head comfortable and supported).

2) Try and make sure the area is positive and cleared of any negative energy; you may like to use a room spray to clear negative or stale energy, or burn white sage or aromatherapy oils.

You may also like to work with Archangel Raphael's crystals (either clear quartz or emerald or both), simply hold the crystals in your hand or have them beside you.

3) Have a candle lighting if in a room setting and soft music playing.

4) Just breathe gently in your own time and space, inhaling and exhaling three times, now feel your body start to slowly relax.

5) Imagine tiny roots or little flowers coming down from the soles of your feet, pushing through the floor into the ground.

6) Start to visualise a golden ray of light, pouring into the room, see this light shining over you from the top of your head to the bottom of your feet.

7) Breathe in this golden light and let this golden light fill up every cell in your body. Sense your mind becoming very wise and calm and your body absorbing this golden light; let it fill you with energy and vitality.

8) Let the golden light fill up the room or place you are in; it's as if you are sitting in a golden bubble of light.

9) Call in your guardian angel now, "Blessed Guardian Angel be at my side" (or whatever you feel comfortable saying) and visualise your Guardian Angel coming into the room lovingly to work with you.

10) Let your Guardian Angel place its light and heavenly wings around you. Lie back now in your Angel's loving embrace.

11) When you are ready take your Guardian Angels hand and walk out of the room, imagine or visualise yourself out in nature, walking thorough the emerald green grass with the sun shining down forming small rays of light all around you. The sky is a light blue colour: breathe in this blue and feel the light breeze on your face; enjoy the peace and perfection around you.

As you walk through the emerald green grass, become aware of the small wild flowers, butterflies, bees; feel God our Creator with you through the presence of Mother Nature. It's as if you are one, with everything present.

12) As you walk with your Guardian Angel, you might find yourself sharing a joke or story with your angel, or even listening to your angel's wisdom. If you need a question answered just ask your angel and the answer may come very clearly. Or it may come just as a whisper, or in pictures. The answer can even come later on, when you least expect it (sometimes when we let go the right answer comes).

13) See yourself walking through the grass with your Guardian Angel at your side. In the distance you see a little gate and you tell your angel that you would like to see where the gate leads.

14) Go up and open the gate, walk through it into a beautiful large garden. There are lots of trees, flowers, plants, shrubs, even wild-flowers; just visualise all your favourite flowers (lilies, roses, daffodils, irises, or whatever you like).

15) Everything seems so vivid and bright in the garden. Let all the colours fill your mind and senses, the blue sky, the emerald green grass, the sound of the trees swaying, the colourful array of flowers. It's just so peaceful, a bit like heaven on earth.

16) As you walk around the garden, the golden sun-light seems to pour all around you, guiding you, supporting you; you feel very blessed.

17) As you come to the end of the garden, you see a lovely waterfall. The water is crystal clear and very inviting. You feel very drawn to the waterfall so you go over to look at it; it's not too deep, so with your Guardian Angel's help, you now stand under the waterfall.

18) Let this beautiful clear divine healing water, pour over you; the water feels so soothing and healing. As the water washes over you, start to release all fears, anxieties and worries into the waterfall. Let go of them now and see the water dissolving them away gently.

19) You now feel completely free and an incredible sense of peace and love engulf you. The golden sunlight just pours

through the waterfall, starting to form little rainbows of light all around you. As you breathe in this light, you feel wonderful.

20) When you are ready, step out of the waterfall and let the golden sunlight dry you off. Now get a sense of a magnificent loving and healing presence approaching you, surrounded in gold and emerald green light. This is Archangel Raphael the supreme healing Archangel.

21) Archangel Raphael, places his emerald green healing light around you. You feel so good, so nurtured and happy.

22) Take Archangel Raphael's hand and let Raphael lead you to a beautiful soft white arm chair with a foot and head rest. Sit in this chair and get a sense of Archangel Raphael, continually pouring his loving emerald green healing light over you now. Absorb this light and if you need any physical or emotional healing ask Archangel Raphael now to help you (or if anyone you know needs healing or an animal or pet).

23) If you would like to have a career in helping or healing people, ask Archangel Raphael now to put the right healing, holistic or medical course your way and if you need abundance for your course or to start your healing centre, ask Archangel Raphael to help you.

24) If you would like to have a holiday, or you need help with your travel plans, ask Archangel Raphael to help. If you are looking for the right home, ask Archangel Raphael to show you the right place to live. You can even tell Raphael your deepest secrets or fears and this wonderful healing Archangel, will always listen and support you.

25) When you have finished talking to Archangel Raphael, thank Raphael for all his help and support. Then take your Guardian Angel's hand and leave this heavenly garden, knowing that at any time you can return back there to work with Archangel Raphael and all the healing angels.

26) Visualise yourself walking out of the gate and back into the countryside; everything seems lighter, happier, and more serene.

27) Let your blessed Guardian Angel lead you back into the space where you started from.

28) See the little flowers or roots coming gently up from the ground back into the soles of your feet, your feet feel grounded and balanced.

29) Get a sense of your upper and lower body in the chair or bed and start to breathe gently, then stretch out, move your body and get up in your own time.

30) Blow out any candles and go about your day, knowing that Archangel Raphael is by your side.

Archangel Raphael Story

I have found down through the years, that my experiences with Archangel Raphael have been life changing and often miraculous. Raphael was one of the first Archangels that came into my life back in 1997, when I reconnected back with the angelic realm, as I experienced a wonderful healing in my life both physically and emotionally.

Now I work with Archangel Raphael on a daily basis, as Raphael often accompanies me on my client appointments. The connection I feel to Archangel Raphael goes beyond description; it is a spiritual connection of times past, present and future.

Archangel Raphael has truly been one of my spiritual mentors and guides here on the earth, constantly enlightening and supporting me, whilst teaching me along the way. Archangel Raphael has supported me through thick and thin, even when I felt challenged by life, other people and my own feelings.

For me, Archangel Raphael's gentle healing light is one of the most powerful experiences a person can have, as well as one of the most uplifting. The reality is that we all need some sort of healing from time to time as human beings living on planet Earth, whether it's emotional, physical or spiritual. Often when we call upon Archangel Raphael he can step in and be our healing knight with his emerald green light (which is a direct healing line to God our Creator).

Probably my most important encounter with Archangel Raphael was about eleven years ago. At the time I felt very run down, as I had been busy and stressed out with a new job. I was at home not feeling very well. My temperature was high and I felt very warm, I also had a nagging pain in my stomach. I rang my sister who came and called the doctor on call. He seemed worried and advised me to go into casualty, so we did. When I got to the hospital I felt so weak that I couldn't stand up properly. I was placed on a trolley in the casualty ward and as I lay there, I got a sense of my body becoming weaker and weaker, like I was starting to sink.

I called in my angels and I asked Archangel Raphael to be with me, but I still felt weak. I asked for a sign and a lovely nurse with very golden curly hair came towards me and seemed genuinely concerned. She looked a bit like the actress 'Meg Ryan' from the film "City of Angels". I had watched "City of Angels", about a week or so before, so I felt strangely comforted when I saw her. I then heard the nurse and doctor say that I was very run down and I had a suspected kidney infection, but they were the most worried about my temperature and kept trying to get it back to normal.

But what happened in the next few moments, was about to change my whole perspective on life. My body seemed to become weaker and weaker - "This is it", I thought and fear crept silently over me. I decided "to let go and let God take care of me", as I slowly closed my eyes an incredible feeling of pure peace came over me - it was like nothing on the earth that I had ever experienced before.

I felt wonderful, ecstatic, completely unconditionally loved. Then as I opened my eyes, I felt as if I were next to the ceiling, looking down at my body. I was a little surprised at first, but it felt completely normal to me, as if this was my true self. A bright misty light seemed to gather around me, which again felt normal and was very comforting. I could have stayed in this loving light all night.

As I lay back in this wonderful light, looking down at my body, I immediately got a sense of a voice that was not above me but within me. It was a very calm, loving voice, completely reassuring and it seemed quite wise and definite. It was concerned that I should return back to my original body and gently asked me to return. As soon as I connected with this voice, I was back in my body. The nurse told me that my temperature was returning to normal. I was then transferred to another hospital where they did tests and I stayed there most of the night. The next day I was simply sent home, as I felt a lot better.

In the days and weeks that followed, I experienced only feelings of pure peace and unconditional love. In fact everywhere I went life seemed so vivid, flowers were colourful, landscapes seemed bright and welcoming. I felt completely connected to Mother Nature and all of life. It was an amazing feeling, like being in heaven. My experience lasted for about two weeks and by the time it ended I had completely recovered.

I now know that I was given a glimpse of heaven, as my spirit had left my body for just a brief moment, yet I was guided back. I also know that Archangel Raphael and the healing angels helped me heal, that night, as they were guided by God our Creator. This experience has helped me become closer to God and the angels, for I know in my heart and soul that we are all part of this loving universe and we are all deeply loved and supported unconditionally by God and the Angels.

Chapter 8

Archangel Michael

Archangel Michael: is one of the main Archangels and is said to be one of the closest Archangels to God our Creator. Archangel Michael is the Archangel most spoken about in religious books or texts. The name Michael means "He who is like God". Archangel Michael is the Archangel of protection, peace, safety, clarity and moving forward.

Archangel Michael is also known as the supreme protector giving us strength and courage. He is often called the "Prince of Light", the chief fighter against negativity. Michael is a warrior angel, commanding legions of warrior angels to help us in times of fear.

Archangel Michael is very strong, kind and direct. Michael's energy is very grounded and present, completely connected to God's unconditional love. It is said in astrology that Archangel Michael is associated with the fire signs: Aries, Leo, and Sagittarius.

Description: Archangel Michael is said to have a deep blue light around him, that is his protective shield and Archangel Michael is often depicted carrying a golden sword of light. This sword is a healing sword of light and is used to cut through any negative energy, cords, or fears, surrounding a person or situation, often bringing instant healing and clarity.

Aura: very golden, strong bright light, deep blue aura.

Colours: gold, deep blue and sometimes strong purple.

Symbol: golden sword of light, protective shield, amulet, spear, strong wind, speed, deep blue or golden feather.

Animal: golden eagle, elephant, bear, leopard, horse.

Crystal: lapis lazuli, blue sapphire, smoky quartz, citrine (all can be in crystals, tumbled stones, or jewellery form).

Lapis Lazuli: deep blue stone with gold flecks, a protector stone or crystal, the stone of peace and letting go.

Blue Sapphire: often bright blue or violet blue in colour. It can be good for holding your spiritual centre, even releasing the past and creating peace. It is often cut or faceted into jewellery.

Smoky Quartz: a light or dark brown crystal or stone, it is said to protect against psychic attack. It is also very grounding and is seen as a stone of clarity.

Citrine: golden clear crystal, good for energy, abundance, strength and enthusiasm.

Flower Essence: *Walnut:* for grounding, strength, courage, protection, moving forward, cutting cords, freedom from attachments, new beginnings.

Working Together: we can call upon Archangel Michael if we feel afraid or need protection, as Archangel Michael will put his deep blue light around us, bringing us comfort and support. We can also ask Archangel Michael to give us clarity and show us the truth, regarding any situation. Michael often brings justice, peace and balance into our lives and can give us the confidence, strength and courage to move forward in life.

How to Work with Archangel Michael

I feel we can all work with Archangel Michael, as he will always answer our call in the best possible way. When we invoke the presence of Archangel Michael, we may feel a strong yet loving presence. I often get a sense of a strong breeze as Archangel Michael enters the room. Michael often moves swiftly, on a golden ray of light surrounded in deep blue.

People often tell me, that when they call upon Archangel Michael, they feel instantly safe and protected and have great peace of mind.

Situations when to call upon Archangel Michael:

1) If you are feeling lonely or in despair.

2) If you feel scared and frightened.

3) If you need courage or protection.

4) If your life or a situation needs clarity or focus.

5) If you want to cut the cords to a negative person or a situation in your life, so you can move on (this is only done by Archangel Michael in a loving healing way for the higher good of both parties involved).

6) If you are being attacked, either verbally, physically, sexually, or psychically.

7) If you need to be direct or speak out.

8) If you are fighting a situation of injustice.

9) If you need to send loved ones protection.

10) If you are coping with change in your life, and you need the courage to move forward.

11) If you need to develop leadership qualities and be successful (Archangel Michael is said to have worked with Joan of Arc and is often present with the great Spiritual and Political Leaders (past and present) i.e.: Nelson Mandela, President Obama and the late Martin Luther King and Ghandi).

12) If you are being spiritual persecuted.

13) For energy and enthusiasm.

This is a quick meditation to do with Archangel Michael, so you feel safe and supported.

Archangel Michael Meditation
(Blue light of protection)

1) Find a nice space to work in, sit in a nice comfortable chair or if lying down make sure your head is supported.

2) Imagine tiny roots coming down from the soles of your feet, pushing into the ground below, so your feet feel safe and protected.

3) Now see a golden circle of light from heaven pouring around you, it's as if you are sitting in this golden circle.

4) Call in Archangel Michael; you might like to say "Archangel Michael work with me today" or "Archangel Michael be at my side."

5) Visualise Archangel Michael, moving swiftly on a golden ray of light with his sword and blue light and imagine Archangel Michael putting his "strong blue light" around you for protection.

6) Then ask Archangel Michael, for whatever help you need, you can even visualise Archangel Michael with his sword of light, simply cutting away or dissolving any negativity in your life. Then ask Archangel Michael for the strength and courage to follow your divine life path.

7) Visualise or imagine Archangel Michael sending in his heavenly angels to help you and a golden light from heaven pouring around you. Just know that everything is being looked after right now.

8) Then say "thank you" to Archangel Michael and believe that the situation is already being taken care of. You might like to say, "I am safe and protected now and always."

9) Then during the day and evening, just continue to surround yourself with Archangel Michael's strong blue light.

10) Trust now that Archangel Michael and his group of angels are looking after you.

You can ask Archangel Michael:

1) To put you, in His blue protective light and keep you safe.

2) Pour golden heavenly light down on you and any situation.

3) To help cut away any negative energy with his golden sword of light.

Affirmations and Prayers to Archangel Michael

"Archangel Michael protect me now".

"Archangel Michael surround me with your blue light and keep me safe".

"Archangel Michael give me clarity, show me where to go and what to do".

"Archangel Michael give me the strength and courage I need right now".

"Archangel Michael give me confidence".

(Thank you).

Remember: it is very important to thank Archangel Michael after your affirmations, prayers, or written requests, as gratitude helps show we believe, then just trust and let go.

The following visualisation can help you connect with Archangel Michael, in a wonderful positive way, helping you let go of any fears or worries. As Archangel Michael can free you from situations in your life that have kept you down, helping you move forward in a more positive way.

You can also ask Archangel Michael for guidance, to show you what to do next or where to go. As Archangel Michael can help you find the necessary confidence, courage and protection to move forward in life.

Visualisation with Archangel Michael

1) Find a comfortable space to visualise in (you can lie or sit down, if lying down keep your head comfortable and supported).

2) Make sure wherever you are, the area is positive and cleared of any negative energy. You might like to work with Archangel Michael's crystals, either hold the crystals in your hand or have them beside you (Archangel Michael's crystals are lapis lazuli, smoky quartz, blue sapphire and golden citrine). If you wish,

you can also use a room spray to clear any negative or stale energy or even burn white sage or aromatherapy oils.

3) Light a candle and play soft music.

4) Some people like to have an Archangel Michael statue or picture beside them (a friend of mine likes to write "Archangel Michael", out on a piece of paper and put it in her bag or purse for a feeling of safety).

5) People sometimes like to be out in nature when they visualise with Archangel Michael, maybe near a river, lake, sea shore or by strong trees. It is entirely up to you (I do however find myself very connected to Archangel Michael in rooms with a strong blue colour or in medieval churches with stain glass windows or walking up small mountains, hills or beside trees or lakes).

6) Remember Archangel Michael, will work with you anywhere and at anytime, you just have to believe that's all.

7) When you are ready to begin, take three gentle deep breaths and exhale after each breath. Feel the peace around you and imagine very strong little roots or flowers coming down from the soles of your feet, pushing into the ground, your feet feel strong and grounded.

8) You may at this stage want to call in your Guardian Angel; you can simply say "My Guardian Angel work with me today."

9) Now imagine or visualise, a strong golden light pouring into the room or around you if out in nature. Let this golden light fall gently over you, a bit like a shower of golden heavenly light.

10) Breathe in this golden light, let it fill your body, mind and senses and let this light surround you in a circle of golden light.

11) Imagine the golden light, getting stronger and brighter around you. Just relax back in the golden light and let yourself be nurtured and supported.

12) Visualise yourself and your Guardian Angel walking in the woods or a small forest. The sky is very blue and the golden sunlight is shinning through the trees, forming rays of light all around you. Just walk through the forest or woods following the light.

13) You feel very comfortable and safe, knowing your Guardian Angel is by your side. Start to breathe in the beauty all around you, the strong earthy trees, scent of the wood, the peace. It's as if you are in harmony with all of your surroundings and there is no separation.

14) As you walk through the forest, a sense of familiarity descends upon you; it's as if all your ancestors and the angels are watching over you.

15) You come to the edge of the forest or wood with your guardian angel, then you step out onto the green grass .As you walk through the grass, you see in the distance a beautiful deep blue river and you tell your angel you would like to visit this river.

16) Walk towards this deep blue river and notice the clear blue colour of the water. Listen to the gentle rustle of the water and feel the calmness around you.

17) Imagine a lovely blue armchair by the river, and just sit there, breathing in all this goodness.

18) Relax back in this comfy supportive blue chair and sink into its loving embrace.

19) Observe the calmness of the water, its clear blue colour filling your mind. Then after a while you start to get a sense of a great presence and the water starts to form ripples moving faster.

20) Archangel Michael, slowly appears now surrounded in blue and golden light. Michael is dressed in deep blue robes, holding a golden sword of healing light.

21) You feel very safe and protected.

22) Archangel Michael pours his deep blue light around you now.

23) Imagine Archangel Michael, as a good friend now and simply talk to him, especially if you need strength or courage or if you are facing a challenge in your life, hand it all over to him.

24) Trust that Archangel Michael, is listening to you, and is taking care of everything.

25) You can even ask Archangel Michael, for the strength and courage to move forward, in your life now.

26) If there is a situation or even someone in your life, that is constantly draining or bullying you or keeping you down. Then

in a loving positive way, you can ask Archangel Michael to cut or dissolve the cords (the emotional attachment to this situation).

27) Imagine one end of a rope tied around you and then the other end of the rope tied around the person or situation with which you are having difficulty. Then visualise Archangel Michael standing in the middle of the rope between you and the person or situation.

28) Ask Archangel Michael, on your behalf to help you cut the cords to this person or situation. So you both can be free and move on; ask for this to be done in a loving healing way, that's best for you both.

29) See Archangel Michael with his golden sword of light, three times cutting the imaginary rope or cord that binds you.

30) Let a healing occur and see yourself free from this person or situation. Hand the whole thing over to Archangel Michael, for the highest good of all concerned.

31) Visualise Archangel Michael, putting you in his blue light, let peace and harmony surround you.

32) Thank Archangel Michael, and see Archangel Michael starting to leave, wave goodbye now.

33) Know that at anytime, you can come back to this river and work with Archangel Michael.

34) Take your Guardian Angel's hand and walk back through the woods or forest, following the light.

35) Your Guardian Angel brings you back into the space that you started from.

36) See the little roots or flowers coming up from the ground back into the soles of your feet, your feet feel strong and grounded.

37) Get a sense of your upper and lower body, present in the chair or wherever you are lying down.

38) Now flex and stretch your body, then breathing gently count from one to seven and get up when you are ready.

39) Blow out any candles, and then go about your day, knowing that Archangel Michael is with you.

Archangel Michael Story

The first time, I truly connected with Archangel Michael, was when I was living in Dublin. I remember it clearly, as it was a lovely summer's evening in June of 1998. I was happily munching my sandwich and sipping my latte in the park at St. Stephen's Green, Dublin, after work. I was reading an angel book at the time and a young couple had just sat down on the wooden bench beside me. I remember the sky was very blue and the sun was shining, it was truly blissful.

As I took a deep breath in, I absorbed the beauty of Mother Nature all around me. I truly felt deeply satisfied to be here in my own private space - it was just heavenly. Then suddenly out of nowhere, a fearful feeling started to come over me, a dark sense of impending danger. From my past experiences, I have learnt to listen to my intuitive feelings, as I know that the angels often work with us through our feelings and intuition and in my case I have always felt this in my solar plexus (stomach area).

I turned to look at the young couple to my left, but they were oblivious in each others arms. I then looked to my right but there was nothing. "Could I be mistaken?" I wondered, as I prayed silently to my angels.

As I opened my eyes, the fearful feelings started to return once again and now looking straight ahead, I saw the truth: a very tall, tattooed, scary looking man was ten yards in front of me. As I meekly scanned his aura, all I could see was a grey black cloud over his head with red, lots of murky dark red. I knew then he was a junkie and I froze, knowing that my handbag, with everything in it but the kitchen sink, was beneath my feet and yet I still couldn't move. All the work with my angels and with Archangel Michael still couldn't prepare me for this moment.

My world had simply stopped, as if in slow motion and everything around me seemed to deliberately animate in sequence - I was terrified. When the body and mind go into shock or fright, it's as if you leave your body and you view everything through a silent screen, a bit like Alice through the looking glass. Here I was, experiencing my own fear, through a distant separate reality, but my body was still on the park bench and as much as I tried, I simply couldn't move or speak.

The tall figure came towards me with confident, yet menacing strides. He then reached down and took a hold of my hand bag. This jolted me back into focus, as I blinked wide eyed from fright just staring at him with pleading eyes. He gave me a slight down turn of a smile, as if to say "like taking sweets from a child" - it was so, so easy for him. As I closed my eyes, tears of terror rolled down my cheeks - it had all happened so fast, in split seconds. Deep in my mind, I cried out "Archangel Michael please help me".

And a strange occurrence then took place; looking back it was really a true miracle. As soon as I thought, "Archangel Michael help me", my terrifying assailant who was by now at least twenty yards away, seemed to stare above him directly into space, with a bemused yet shocked look on his face.

This man then very calmly and slowly, walked back over to me and handed me back my handbag, with all its original items inside - purse, money, keys, cards etc. He muttered a feeble "sorry"! and then he simply took off - he ran like the wind. Never have I seen someone run that fast.

When what actually happened to me began to sink in. I realised it was "Archangel Michael" and his warrior angels of light protecting me. The ironic thing was when I turned the next page of the angel book, I had been reading, there was an amazing picture of Archangel Michael.

When I arrived home, later on that evening, there was a definite blue light fading in and out of my little studio apartment - it felt so peaceful and safe. This light seemed to stay with me, until I fell fast asleep and when I woke up, I felt very protected and happy. Thank you Archangel Michael.

Chapter 9

Archangel Uriel

Archangel Uriel: means "wisdom of God" and is known as the wise Archangel that can illuminate and light our way. Archangel Uriel is said to shine his lantern of light and wisdom on any situation, providing us with an instant solution.

Archangel Uriel is the Archangel of work, justice, fairness and trust and is often associated with political knowledge and reform. Uriel can help large organisations remain balanced and grounded. Archangel Uriel can also help us deal with emotional issues and changes in our life, giving us great subtle insight into situations that trouble us, whilst supporting us emotionally.

Description: Archangel Uriel has an incredible golden energy and is often seen wearing golden amber or brown robes. Archangel Uriel, can also be seen carrying a lantern of light. This lantern of light illuminates our way, by giving us new and bright ideas (especially in the morning). Archangel Uriel is said to very wise and have a gentle peaceful expression, radiating truth and unconditional love wherever he goes. Archangel Uriel is the patron of all the earth signs (Virgo, Taurus, and Capricorn).

Aura: Very golden and bright, orange, golden brown, radiating divine light and wisdom.

Colours: gold, brown, amber, orange light.

Symbol: lantern, brown robes, scroll, woods, sun at dusk and dawn, light pouring through the clouds, golden orange feather.

Animal: owl, stag, salmon.

Crystals: carnelian, amber, rutilated quartz.

Carnelian: can be brown orange and terracotta in colour. It is a very grounding stone. Carnelian can also bring clarity and focus to any situation and can help balance the emotions. Carnelian can be tumbled and in point form or made into jewellery and is often used as a palm stone for comfort.

Rutilated Quartz: is a clear golden brown type crystal, often with reddish or thin dark strands or lines running through the crystal. It is said to facilitate spiritual guidance and is known as a keeper of balance. It can help us see the cause or root of our problems. Rutilated quartz is said to act as a protector, whilst bringing in the light and is associated with wisdom of the ancestors.

Amber: is said to be one of the wise crystals and is also very grounding and protective, as it protects, revitalises and cleanses. Amber is great for the emotions, mind, body and spirit and is said to help you connect to the ancestors and past lives.

Flower Essence: *Wild Oat:* can help us feel focused, giving us clarity. It is a very grounding flower essence and is said to be of assistance in helping us attract or select a new career or job.

Working Together: When we need help or focus we can invoke or work with Archangel Uriel, especially if a situation needs clarity. Archangel Uriel will shine his lantern of light on the situation, enlightening us and showing us what to do. Archangel Uriel can also create wonderful solutions to our problems, alleviating any worries we may have. As the Archangel of work, he can help us find a new job, or improve our existing working conditions. You can also call upon Archangel Uriel in situations of injustice, or if you need balance or peace in your life.

Working with Archangel Uriel

Archangel Uriel is considered to be one of the Archangels of wisdom and is said to illuminate your mind, giving you wisdom and clarity. For me, Archangel Uriel is a wise sage that often lights my way, helping me create wonderful solutions in my life.

Archangel Uriel is considered to be an important Archangel appearing subtly at first, with a gentle golden serene presence. Archangel Uriel can help us find our focus, by illuminating situations with his lantern of light, so we find the perfect solution.

Archangel Uriel's presence is grounding and comforting. Archangel Uriel can provide us with the clarity that we need to move forward in life. In work situations people often look to Archangel Uriel for practical and down to earth advice, as once called upon, Archangel Uriel, will shine his immense golden light upon any issue bringing about clear results.

If you are ever in stormy weather, or worried about the weather (thunder, lighting, heavy rainfall) call upon Archangel Uriel for assistance, as Uriel is considered one of the angels of the weather.

You can ask Archangel Uriel:

1) To help you find a new job or the right job for you.

2) To give you wisdom, balance and clarity about any situation.

3) Shine his lantern of light down on you, to help you move forward illuminating your path along the way.

4) Help provide an instant solution to any political situation or injustice.

5) Help you to stay real (true to yourself) and grounded.

The following meditation with Archangel Uriel, is for wisdom, especially in relation to all work situations.

Meditation with Archangel Uriel
(For finding a new job or healing a current work situation)

1) Find a comfortable space to sit or lie down in and make sure your head is supported.

2) You might like to have a candle lighting or some nice music playing.

3) Take three deep gentle breaths, inhale and exhale with each breath.

4) Then just breathe gently in your own time and start to unwind and relax.

5) Imagine or visualise, tiny little roots or flowers coming down from the soles of your feet, pushing into the ground.

6) Your feet feel very strong and safe.

7) Imagine a golden light, a bit like a golden mist of light coming into the room. Let this light shimmer and dissolve gently over you.

8) Breathe in this golden light, let it fill your mind and body.

9) Call in Archangel Uriel: you might like to say "Blessed Archangel Uriel, light my way and help me find the right job" (specify what kind of job you want and be clear or simply ask for guidance to be put on the right career path). If you need help and guidance with your current job, just tell Archangel Uriel about it and hand it over.

10) If you want to change your job or work, ask Archangel Uriel to help you do this. As Archangel Uriel will bring you to the right people you need to meet or the places you need to be in and even guide you to look at certain news papers, agencies, internet work sites etc.

11) Archangel Uriel, will help you with your job interview often helping you prepare during the interview.

12) Visualise Archangel Uriel, opening all the doors and shining his lantern of light on your career path, helping you create your Divine life's work.

13) Now get a sense of this golden light, illuminating your life and work. See everything as balanced and in harmony.

14) You can even do this meditation, to help someone else find the right work or job.

15) When you are ready, then thank Archangel Uriel, just believe and trust that things are working out now for you.

16) Get a sense of yourself back in the space from where you started from, breathe gently now.

17) Let the little roots or flowers come slowly up from the ground, back into the soles of your feet.

18) Feel good, ready to move forward. Slowly flex your body and muscles and get up.

19) Blow out the candle, turn off the music and go about your day in peace, knowing that Archangel Uriel is at your side.

As Archangel Uriel is a very wise, grounding and earthy Archangel, I often find it wonderful to work with Archangel Uriel out in nature, especially near trees or woods. I like to sit near trees with my back against a tree for support. As I find this very grounding. Also if the grass is clean and dry, I often take my shoes off, as I find I can connect easier to Mother Nature. This for me heightens my connection to Archangel Uriel and also the angels of nature (fairies, elementals).

I also often wear or hold various crystals in my hand, with Archangel Uriel I would mainly work with carnelian or amber or rutilated quartz. If I am out in nature by trees, rutilated quartz and amber can help connect you to the ancestors (as the Celts and druids were very associated with trees). Amber is made from tree sap or resin that has become fossilised down through the years. Many people often feel that amber contains the cell memory of our ancestors, who lived near or worked with trees.

Rutilated Quartz is thought to be of help in relation to helping us access cell memory through its thin strands, which is thought to facilitate Divine Light to pass through. It has been said that rutilated quartz can help us access the past, present and future, whilst bringing clarity into our lives.

Affirmations and Prayers to Archangel Uriel

"Archangel Uriel, light my way, today."

"Archangel Uriel, show me what to do."

"Archangel Uriel, open the way for my right job to come today."

"Archangel Uriel, help me find a wonderful new fulfilling job."

"Archangel Uriel, shine your lantern of light in front of me and help me with the following situation ....."

"Archangel Uriel, bring many inspired ideas to me now and let me find an instant solution to......(state your request)."

"Archangel Uriel, keep me balanced and grounded now."

(Thank you).

Remember: It is very important to thank Archangel Uriel, after your affirmations, prayers or written requests believing in the highest outcome for yourself and others.

The following visualisation can help you connect directly with Archangel Uriel. As Archangel Uriel is the Archangel that deals with emotional and work related issues.

When we work with Archangel Uriel, we can ask him to help create political reform in any work situation or organisation or even ask for help in finding the right job.

If you are facing a situation of injustice work-wise, then Archangel Uriel will then shine his lantern of light on the situation and give you the courage to move forward, making the necessary changes.

Archangel Uriel is a wise and subtle Archangel, often giving us great insight into situations that trouble us, whilst supporting us emotionally by helping us remain grounded and balanced. It is also said that Archangel Uriel has an incredible golden light that can help illuminate our way.

Visualisation with Archangel Uriel

1) Find a comfortable space to visualise in, sit or lie down, (if lying down keep your head comfortable and supported) or if you prefer, go out to nature or sit by trees.

2) Make sure the area is positive and cleared of any negative energy, you might like to work with Archangel Uriel's crystals, either hold the crystals in your hand or have them beside you (Archangel Uriel's crystals are carnelian, amber and rutilated quartz) you may like to use a room spray to clear negative or stale energy or burn white sage or aromatherapy oils.

3) Have a candle lighting, if you are in a room setting (only) or maybe have soft music playing.

4) Breathe gently, in your own time and space, inhaling and exhaling three times, now feel your body start to slowly relax.

5) Imagine tiny little roots or flowers coming down from the soles of your feet, pushing through the floor and spreading out all over the ground below.

6) Visualise a ray of golden light pouring into the room or where you are out in nature and see this light shining over you, from the top of your head to the bottom of your feet Breathe in this light.

7) Let this golden light fill up every part of you and sense your mind becoming very wise and calm, visualise your body absorbing this golden light and let it fill up every cell in your body with energy and vitality.

8) Let the golden light fill up the room or place you are in. See the room as very golden, as if you are sitting in a golden bubble of light.

9) Call in your Guardian Angel, you can say "Guardian Angel be at my side" (or whatever you feel comfortable saying).

10) Let your Guardian Angel place its heavenly wings around you and lie back now in your angel's loving embrace.

11) When you are ready take your Guardian Angel's hand and walk out of the room. Imagine or visualise yourself out in nature, walking thorough emerald green grass, the sun is shining forming small rays of light all around you.

The sky is a soft light blue colour, breathe in this blue colour, feel the light breeze on your face as you enjoy the peace and perfection around you. Walk through the emerald green grass and become aware of everything the small wild flowers, butterflies, bees, feel all of Mother Nature, life, God our Creator, the universal energy around you. It's as if, you are one with everything present.

12) In the distance you see a small wood or forest and you tell your angel that you would like to go in there. As you approach the wood or forest, everything seems so still, serene, peaceful, it's as if time has stood still for you. Even each tree seems to tell

its own story, as the leaves are beautiful, lots of reds, browns, orange and golden leaves.

13) Find a tree that you feel connected to and sit down with your back against the tree, absorb the beauty and peace around you.

14) Visualise small rays of golden sunlight starting to filter through the trees, shining directly down on you, let the golden sunlight pour gently over you now.

15) Suddenly, you get a sense of an amber golden light coming towards you, as it gets nearer it seems to get brighter and brighter and you sense a wise loving presence beside you.

16) Archangel Uriel then appears surrounded in amber robes with a golden aura or halo of light around him. In his right hand, Archangel Uriel holds a wonderful golden lantern of light in front of him, illuminating his path.

17) Visualise Archangel Uriel's golden light, falling softly over you and breathe in this golden wise light. Let it fill your mind body and senses, so you feel completely safe and supported in this light now.

18) Just talk to Archangel Uriel, especially if you need help with a work project or if you need a solution to a particular problem that is bothering you. Even if you need wisdom or insight, hand the problem over to Archangel Uriel now.

19) You might like to say, " Archangel Uriel help me find a solution to ....." or " Archangel Uriel light my way now and show me what to do ..." or "Archangel Uriel shine your lantern of

light my way and help move me forward in my life especially in the area of .....".

20) Visualise Archangel Uriel shining his lantern of light on whatever issue needs clarity or healing in your life and see the problem being resolved.

21) Trust that everything is being taken care of now.

22) When you are ready say goodbye to Archangel Uriel, knowing that his wisdom and light is supporting you now, you are very blessed.

24) Relax back under the tree and thank Archangel Uriel and your guardian angel and all the ancestors for their help today.

25) Then take your Guardian Angel's hand and leave this beautiful forest or woods, knowing that you can return back there at any time.

26) Walk out of the wood or forest and come back out into the countryside, feel the peace all around you.

27) Let your Guardian Angel lead you back to the space from where you started from.

28) Now visualise the little roots or flowers coming slowly up from the ground, back into the soles of your feet. Your feet feel very grounded, your body feels relaxed and present.

29) Breathe gently now, in your own time and space and get a sense that you are back in your space and your Guardian Angel is at your side.

30) Open your eyes and stretch slowly, flexing your muscles. Then blow out any candles and go about your day, knowing that Archangel Uriel is supporting you now.

Archangel Uriel Story

I have often called upon Archangel Uriel, to help guide and enlighten me and put me on the right track in my work.

I now include the following true story.

In Autumn of 2002 I had moved to a small town in the U.K. called Leamington Spa. I was working and studying at the time and I had a job in a small shop that sold candles, oils, angel statues and various holistic products. Even though it was a nice place, the job was not well paid. As I was studying at the time, I often found this difficult to manage with bills and rent to pay.

After one particularly trying day, I decided to go for a walk to the local park on my lunch break. The sun was shining all around me and it was just so beautiful and serene. I knew in my heart, that I really needed to change jobs, so I began to meditate for a while with my angels, calling in Archangel Uriel for enlightenment. After a few minutes, I began to get a sense of a very golden light around me and I felt safe and grounded. It was as if Archangel Uriel was standing beside me dressed in golden robes.

I told Archangel Uriel, about my current work situation and I asked Archangel Uriel to help me find a new job. Then I handed my request over and within a few minutes the local health food shop flashed into my mind. I thought that was strange, as I had passed by the health food shop earlier that morning and there were no vacancies advertised. However, I have long learnt to listen to my intuition, as prayer and requests, really is us talking with our angels and spiritual guides. Also our angels and spiritual guides can often send us a message back down through our feelings and intuition.

So I decided to call into the health food shop, on my way back from lunch and surprisingly, they had only just put up a sign in the window looking for a second assistant manager. I applied for the job and two weeks later I started working there. "Thank you Archangel Uriel".

I really do feel that Archangel Uriel inspired me to go to the health food shop that day, helping me very subtly by guiding me, whilst opening the door and creating a little miracle for me.

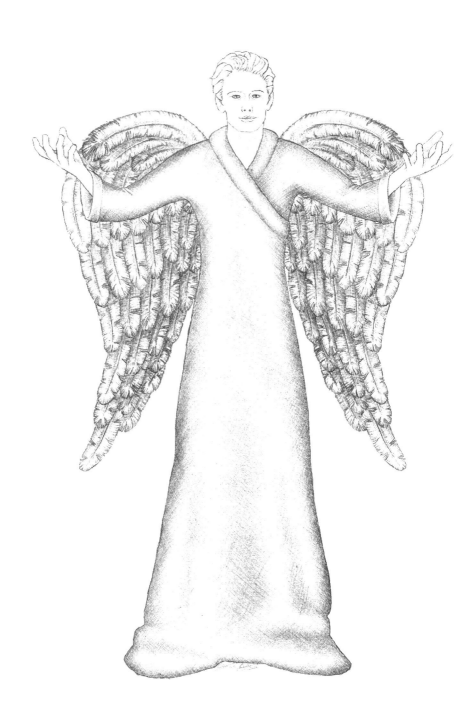

Chapter 10

Archangel Jophiel

Archangel Jophiel: is the "Angel of joy", and is a light filled Archangel, who often works closely with Archangel Uriel.

Archangel Jophiel brings energy renewal, often pouring his golden light energy around us or any situation so we feel lighter and more optimistic about life. It is said that Archangel Jophiel, can help you to let go of the past and create a wonderful new beginning in your life now, bringing in divine joy and bliss.

Archangel Jophiel often works with artists, especially painters and musicians.

Description: A very golden Archangel dressed in light yellow robes with a light golden aura. Archangel Jophiel is a slightly younger looking Archangel radiating a sense of fun, joy, and happiness. When Jophiel steps into the room, it's as if the sun has just come out.

Aura: very golden, yellow and bright light.

Colours: gold, yellow.

Symbol: sun, golden ray of light, field of corn, daffodils, sunflowers, buttercups, candle-flame, fountain, meadow, yellow feather.

Animal: robin, lamb, otter, puppies, humming bird.

Crystal: sunstone and yellow topaz.

Sunstone: is a wonderful positive crystal, as it can uplift you, bringing joy and enthusiasm into your life. I feel sunstone can give your confidence a boost and rejuvenate your energy and your mood, if it is held in the sunshine.

Yellow topaz: can help you feel optimistic and believe in yourself again. It promotes faith and spiritual connections and can often help you feel abundant and generous.

Flower Essence: *Mustard:* is said to help lift the clouds, dispelling doom and gloom, slowly giving us hope, by letting the sun come back in. Mustard flower essence has been known to help a person feel more optimistic.

Working Together: as Archangel Jophiel, is the Archangel of joy, you can work with him at anytime but especially when you are feeling low. Simply invoke Archangel Jophiel and ask him to bring lightness and joy into your life, then things will gently start to improve. It is also good to call upon Archangel Jophiel, if you have a special occasion or celebration, as Jophiel can bring much fun and happiness to it.

If you ever feel blocked or stuck in your life, you can ask Archangel Jophiel to clear away any negative energy and help reboot your life. Archangel Jophiel can help us make a fresh start by bringing in joy and enthusiasm, and also helping us feel motivated, energised, and optimistic about life again.

Working with Archangel Jophiel

Working with Archangel Jophiel, can be a very joyful uplifting experience. Archangel Jophiel can pour his golden yellow ray of light around us, especially if we feel a little bit down or under the weather. Archangel Jophiel can banish the clouds of doom and gloom that can sometimes engulf us, helping us to let go of any worries or anxieties.

Archangel Jophiel has a very gentle, loving happy presence, as his energy is light and subtle. You will instantly know that Archangel Jophiel and the angels of joy are around you, as your mood starts to lift and you feel lighter and happier. When working with Archangel Jophiel, a lovely yellow ray of light will often surround you.

As one of the angels of joy, wisdom, and divine energy Archangel Jophiel often works in unison with Archangel Uriel.

I see Archangel Jophiel, a bit like the younger brother of Archangel Uriel, trailing a yellow golden light around him. When I am out in nature or near a corn field or even wild flowers (daisies and buttercups for example) I am often reminded of Jophiel, because Archangel Jophiel's natural presence is so loving, light and golden. I feel Archangel Jophiel, works very much in harmony with Mother Nature, the elementals and fairies (which are of course the angels of nature).

For me, Archangel Jophiel can help lift our souls up to the heavenly realms by creating a little piece of "heaven on earth" for us, often bringing in joyous energy and helping us to appreciate the simple things in life again, such as smiling, singing, painting and Mother Nature.

It is important to remember, that joy, happiness and laughter, are basic human requirements. It is your human right to feel good, no one has the right to take away your joy or make you feel bad. In fact it's simply impossible, unless you are feeling low in energy and susceptible to negative people or negative energy.

People with negative energy, are what I call "energy vampires" and they can often prey on nice, positive people. For me, they are simply the "joy stealers", who try to steal others joy, sometimes out of desperation or unhappiness, or even insecurity or jealousy. Deep down they are really looking for healing and want to feel good too. The best way to deal with a "joy stealer" or energy vampire is to wish them well and then if you can, casually detach and move on. However, I do know that this can be easier said than done, especially if you are in work or at a social or family occasion.

What I suggest, is that you ask the Archangels to help you, maybe call in Archangel Michael, for protection (see page 51). Then ask Archangel Uriel, for the wisdom to deal with this situation or person, call in Archangel Jophiel to keep you upbeat and positive, as you deal with this issue. Remember do also ask the Archangels that the person in question also receives this goodness too (as everyone needs healing and support even "joy stealers" and "energy vampires").

Archangel Jophiel, can often be seen working with Archangel Uriel, especially in situations of injustice that need balance, wisdom, light and joy. So if you are going through a trying time in your life, you can call in Archangel Jophiel, to lift up the energy, bringing in joy and happiness. Then you can ask Archangel Uriel, for the wisdom and clarity to move forward.

If you know of someone who is going through an injustice, or they simply need more joy and happiness in their life, call upon Archangel Jophiel and Uriel. However, in some cases, you may also need to call upon Archangel Michael, for example in the case of someone who is being very badly bullied or a victim of an injustice. But when these three Archangels band together effectively, real miracles can often occur.

Therefore Archangel Jophiel is a truly wonderful Archangel that can create powerful joyous change in our lives and others.

Archangel Jophiel, can indeed bring true joy and harmony into our lives, so this meditation with Archangel Jophiel is to help us find our true bliss.

Meditation with Archangel Jophiel
(To find your bliss)

1) Find a nice space to sit or lie down in (make sure your head is always supported if lying down).

2) Light a candle.

3) Take three gentle breaths, inhale and exhale with each breath, now start to relax.

4) Then imagine or visualise, tiny little flowers or roots coming down from the soles of your feet, pushing into the ground and spreading out into the soil below, your feet are safe and grounded.

5) Now just relax back and call in Archangel Jophiel.

6) You might like to say "Archangel Jophiel connect with me now; pour joy and happiness into my life."

7) Then in your minds eye (at the centre of your forehead) imagine a divine yellow light and see this yellow light filling your mind and body. Then slowly let this light, fill up the space you are in, breathe in this yellow light and let it totally absorb you.

8) Get a sense of a wonderful light filled Archangel, surrounded in a golden yellow light standing beside you, this is Archangel Jophiel.

9) Now imagine Archangel Jophiel, showering you with his divine yellow light, from the top of your head, right down to the bottom of your feet, experience this joyous light.

10) Let it pour over you, it feels wonderful, blissful, as if all your worries are washed away.

11) If you need joy or happiness in your life, or if someone you know needs to feel good, ask Archangel Jophiel to help direct the joy or bliss, to wherever it is needed and ask Archangel Jophiel to pour his yellow ray of light over you as well.

12) Then hand any worries you have over to Archangel Jophiel and relax back in his blissful light. All you have to do is feel good and you can even ask Archangel Jophiel to help you follow your bliss in life, be it in work or relationships.

13) Then thank Archangel Jophiel, feel light and free as you can now move forward with renewed self confidence and optimism that things are indeed improving.

14) Get a sense of yourself back in the space from where you started from, either sitting in the chair or lying down. Visualise the little flowers or roots coming slowly back up from the ground, into the soles of your feet, your feet feel grounded.

15) Slowly flex your lower and upper body, stretching out if you need to, get up and blow out the candle, go about your day and know Archangel Jophiel's wonderful presence is with you now.

How to work with Archangel Jophiel
You can ask Archangel Jophiel To:

1) Help you follow your bliss.

2) Rejuvenate your life and give you energy.

3) Bring in peace and happiness.

4) Help you stay positive.

5) Surround you with light and energy.

6) Help you remain optimistic despite the outcome.

7) Pour joy and light into your work, especially if you are a painter or musician.

Affirmations and Prayers to Archangel Jophiel

"Archangel Jophiel, pour your golden yellow light of happiness around me."

"Archangel Jophiel, show me how to follow my bliss."

"Archangel Jophiel, help me to stay positive today."

"Archangel Jophiel, put your golden yellow light of inspiration around my creative work."

"Archangel Jophiel, help me to follow the path of the most light."

"Archangel Jophiel, rejuvenate me and my life."

"Archangel Jophiel, lift or dispel, the dark clouds around me now, especially in relation to (describe the person or situation) and let your divine love and light shine through."

(Thank you).

Remember: thank Archangel Jophiel and just believe, trust and let go.

The following visualisation with Archangel Jophiel can help you feel more positive and even help develop your creative talents.

Working and visualising with Archangel Jophiel, can bring a lightness to our life, lifting away any heaviness or negativity.

Visualisation with Archangel Jophiel

1) Find a comfortable space to work in (it can be indoors or outside) clear away any negative or stale energy. If indoors open the window or use some white sage or room sprays, if outside make sure the space is clean and dry where you are sitting.

2) Sit or lie down, keeping your head comfortable and supported.

3) You might like to light a candle or play soft music or work with Archangel Jophiel's crystals: sunstone or yellow topaz, you can hold them in your hand or place them around you, just do whatever works best.

4) Now breathe gently, in your own time and space, inhaling and exhaling three times, feel your body start to relax.

5) Imagine tiny little roots or flowers coming down from the soles of your feet, pushing into the ground below.

6) Visualise a ray of pure white light pouring down on you and let this light gently brush over you, from the top of your head to the bottom of your feet.

7) Breathe in, this white light letting it fill up every part of you with light.

8) Become one with the light.

9) Call in your Guardian Angel. You might like to say: "Blessed Guardian Angel, be at my side", then visualise your Guardian Angel coming into the space where you are.

10) Let your Guardian Angel place its wings around you, and lie back in your angel's loving embrace.

11) When you are ready, take your Guardian Angels hand and walk out of the room, imagine or visualise yourself out in nature walking thorough emerald green grass the sky a lovely light blue colour, breathe in this blue and feel the light breeze on your face, enjoy the peace and perfection around you.

As you walk through the emerald green grass, become aware of everything around you, the small wild flowers, butterflies, bees, feel all of Mother Nature, life, God our Creator, universal energy connecting with you. It's as if you are one with everything present and it is one with you.

12) As the golden sunlight shines down, it forms rays of light all around you. Just follow this light and visualise yourself and your angel walking side by side. In the distance you see a gate and you tell your angel that you would like to go through the gate, to see where it leads.

13) Open the gate and walk through, it seems very bright and you realise that you are in a beautiful golden corn or wheat field. Just walk through the field and be aware of the golden sunlight, shinning brightly, illuminating the whole field. It's so beautiful, as if everything is made from spun gold, shimmering, shinning and golden.

14) Walk through the corn or wheat field and run your hands softly through its crops, absorbing the beauty all around you, feel the gentle sun on your face, it feels as if you are in heaven.

15) Relax back now in this corn field, wheat field and become still. Connect with all the beauty of Mother Nature; everything seems as one in perfect harmony.

17) A glowing yellow light seems to appear beside you, shinning very brightly.

18) As this yellow light, continues to glow and shine around you, let it fill every cell in your body and you begin to feel energised happy and free.

19) Sense a wonderful Archangel standing beside you, dressed in light yellow robes with a very golden light filled aura. This is Archangel Jophiel, the Archangel of divine joy; he seems slightly younger than the other Archangels and has a wonderful

youthful presence radiating happiness light and unconditional love.

20) Archangel Jophiel, just smiles as he sees you and he places his loving bright light yellow around you.

21) Its as if the sun has just come out and is shinning directly down on you, never have you felt such pure unconditional love and happiness. All your worries and anxieties start to dissolve now, as you feel blissful. It's as if you are one with the light and God our Creator.

22) If you want more joy or happiness in your life, ask Archangel Jophiel; if you want to feel renewed, refreshed and optimistic, ask Archangel Jophiel to bring this about for you.

23) If you are an artist or painter or musician you can ask Archangel Jophiel to help you develop your creative talents. Hold a vision of Archangel Jophiel pouring his yellow light, into all of your creative endeavours and see things now really positively moving forward for you. Visualise all your gifts and talents coming up and see yourself receiving the recognition you deserve, bringing joy and happiness to everyone around you.

24) Anything you are worried about, just place in Archangel Jophiel's yellow light, to be healed and rejuvenated.

25) Then thank Archangel Jophiel, just trust and let go. Take your Guardian Angel's hand and very slowly see yourself leaving this beautiful corn or wheat field.

26) Walk back through the gate and out into the countryside with your Guardian Angel at your side.

27) Get a sense of your Guardian Angel leading you back into the space where you started from.

28) See the little flowers or roots coming up gently from the ground, back into the soles of your feet; your feet feel grounded and balanced.

29) Feel your upper and lower body very relaxed and breathe gently, stretch or move your body; then get up in your own time.

30) Blow out any candles and go about your day, knowing that Archangel Jophiel is at your side.

Archangel Jophiel Story

Archangel Jophiel is a wonderful light filled Archangel, who can help us, by lifting our spirits bringing joy into our lives. Archangel Jophiel can even appear in our lives when we least expect it.

I now include the following true story:

About twelve years ago, I was very confused about the way my life was going. At the time I was working in a clothes shop doing retail work and I knew in my heart that it wasn't the right place for me to be working in. I had been doing a lot of overtime at work, which I found very demanding, so I often went home feeling quite drained physically and emotionally.

At the time, I was working so hard, that there seemed little room for joy, rest or even relaxation. It seemed like a never ending cycle. Then early one spring morning, I was in the stock room at work going over the stock, when a waft of sweet, delicious perfume seemed to surround me and I got a distinct feeling that I should just take the day off. However, I knew it was quite busy in the shop that day and it would prove very unfavourable to do so.

However, later on that morning, the sun simply started shinning in through the windows; it was such a beautiful day. "Oh to have some time off" I wished. My head then started to feel a little fuzzy; and I could sense a headache coming on.

The shop just seemed to be getting busier and busier, the sale was on and people were looking for bargains. Then suddenly out of the blue, something extraordinary happened, there was a power cut and everything electrical simply turned off; the lights, the cash registers, the sound system, everything. Our manager then begrudgingly announced to all the staff present, that because we had no electricity at all, we simply had to close up shop for the day.

I was absolutely amazed, yet secretly delighted, as this had never happened before. So I decided to take the day off and go somewhere nice out in nature. Quite near to my house at the time, was a lovely peaceful little park, it had a very Zen feel to it. The park was slightly hidden away in a secluded spot, yet open to the public. But because of my working hours, I hardly ever got time to go there. It was now early on a Tuesday afternoon, so I thought it was the ideal time to visit this park.

As I strolled happily into the park, a great sense of peace seemed to surround me; it was as if time was standing still, everything seemed to gently slow down. I sat down, on a wooden bench nearby and a little robin stopped curiously by singing his heartfelt song, as if welcoming me into this beautiful place. A fragrant smell of cut grass filled my senses and I noticed a soft light breeze, whispering gently through the beech and oak trees. The birds were also singing and the early spring flowers were in bloom. In the distance I heard the sound of school children and cars passing, but I felt very tucked away from the hum drum of life. I was here right now, to heal, rest and rejuvenate.

As I started to relax, I closed my eyes and took several deep breaths. In my mind's eye, a very bright, deep yellow light began to form; this light seemed to waft around me, covering me like a blanket. I let this light start to fill every cell in my body and I suddenly, felt very connected to all of life, as if there was no separation.

Tears of pure joy just poured down my cheeks; I felt so happy! I knew I was being showered with unconditional love and joy; and I felt like a child again, in my own world.

My heart felt totally infused now with happiness. I could feel the light, getting stronger and stronger around me. Then I saw a Divine Archangel standing beside me, surrounded in yellow robes of light. The light was so bright around him, that I could just about make him out. He seemed slightly younger than the other Archangels, I had met before and I realised it was Archangel Jophiel, the Archangel of joy and happiness.

He just smiled at me and told me to hand my worries over to him, so I did, I let go of all the things that had bothered me before and I simply relaxed back in Archangel Jophiel's joyous light.

I felt so peaceful and happy being there, in this wonderful joyous light, that I now started to realise how futile and destructive certain earthly worries or concerns can be and that worry, really is a waste of our time and energy. I now knew that I had become so caught up in my daily routine, that I had let the general complexities of my life take over. Even forgetting, how to simply be myself and yet here was Archangel Jophiel, gently reminding me to take some time out, in Mother Nature.

I truly felt very humbled and grateful to Archangel Jophiel that day, for awakening me, back into my true state of being. I now know that Archangel Jophiel and my Guardian Angel helped create the power cut at work, so that I could have the day off. The saying that "angel's create miracles where there are none", is indeed very true.

Shortly after this experience, new doors began to open for me work wise and my life path began to change as I simply followed my inner guidance.

I now know that when we do not listen to our angel's messages, our angels try to create ways for us to listen, as this is what happened to me.

I always try to remember that day, especially if things are building up again in my life and becoming too hectic for me.

Then I simply take some time out, to nurture my soul and connect back again with my angels.

Chapter 11

Archangel Zadkiel

Archangel Zadkiel: means "righteousness of God" and is one of the principal Archangels in the heavens. Archangel Zadkiel can help us with compassion and forgiveness and is associated with the violet flame, a violet heavenly light that transforms any situation.

Archangel Zadkiel is one of the angels of wisdom, helping us move forward on in this life time. Zadkiel is also known as the keeper of the book of records (a holy book or record of our life's actions and deeds on the earth) and can help us hold fast to our ideals and truth.

Archangel Zadkiel is a lucky Archangel, often said to bring luck and abundance into your life. He can be often seen wearing purple or violet robes of light. Purple being the colour of wealth, richness, authority (that is why Kings, Queens and Clergy often wore purple, it was considered in medieval times that purple brought you closer to God, reserved only for those of higher stature). The truth being we all can wear purple, as it is our divine right to be happy, healthy, loved and abundant on the earth plane and anyone can work with Archangel Zadkiel and the angels of luck and wisdom.

Description: Archangel Zadkiel is said to look very wise and wear very vibrant purple robes. His aura is violet and some people often see Archangel Zadkiel holding a book of records and a cool violet flame of light.

Aura: purple, gold, violet light.

Colours: gold, violet, purple.

Symbol: violet flame, book of records, planet Jupiter, jewels, treasure chest, temple, mountain, violets, iris, purple feather.

Animal: hawk, Siamese cat, peacock, purple butterflies.

Crystals: amethyst and sugalite.

Amethyst: Is an extremely versatile crystal available in all forms, jewellery, crystal points, beds, geodes, stones, palm stones, obelisks and rough rock. Amethyst promotes spiritual growth, helping you align to the divine realms. It's also a protective crystal dispelling negative vibrations. It is cleansing and powerful and in some circles it is considered to be lucky and very creative. One of the master crystals, amethyst can also cleanse and re-charge other crystals.

Sugalite: Is normally violet or purple, in colour and is a very loving, spiritual crystal or stone. It is said to bring qualities of wisdom and compassion to the wearer and can help us find our true purpose here on earth, helping us to be true to ourselves. Sugalite can be fashioned into jewellery or is available in tumbled or in polished form.

Flower Essence: *water violet:* can transmute or dissolve barriers between people, especially if they are self imposed out of shyness or fear. Water violet can promote peacefulness and calmness, helping people develop themselves and move forward with optimism.

Working Together: We can call upon Archangel Zadkiel to help us, make the necessary changes in our lives. Archangel Zadkiel, will put us in his violet flame and helping us move forward, whilst cleansing and healing the past. We can also ask Archangel Zadkiel to bring us luck, success and abundance.

Working with Archangel Zadkiel

Archangel Zadkiel is one of the seven main Archangels and is often thought as the wisest of Archangels. He is said to help us with our journey here on the earth and can oversee all our actions. In biblical terms he is considered to be the keeper of the book of records (our life's deeds).

We can ask Archangel Zadkiel, to help us on our chosen path, giving us the wisdom to succeed. Archangel Zadkiel can also bring us luck and abundance, especially if it is for our divine life purpose.

If you find that life is difficult or that you are at a cross roads in life, or you are constantly repeating the same patterns over and over no matter how hard you try. It's as if you are constantly trudging through mud and you really don't know what to do. Then ask Archangel Zadkiel to intervene and help transform your life.

Archangel Zadkiel is an angel of wisdom and is often associated with karma (our life's deeds past and present). We can ask Archangel Zadkiel to help us let go of the past in a loving way, by transmuting or dissolving past actions.

Archangel Zadkiel is also associated with the colour purple and is often seen wearing purple robes of light. To attract abundance and luck you can ask Archangel Zadkiel to put his purple light around you, as this can certainly help improve your luck, but first of all you must feel you deserve it, as only then will abundance be drawn to you.

Archangel Zadkiel, can bring great compassion and forgiveness into our lives. This is important, especially if you are finding it hard to forgive a person or situation: ask Archangel Zadkiel to help you. It is always important to try and forgive a person who has wronged you with compassion, as forgiveness and compassion can set you free from the deed or situation. However you don't have to agree or condone the wrong doing that has been done to you.

If you truly want to transform your life and move forward in a positive way, then ask Archangel Zadkiel, to put his violet flame of light around you (The violet flame is a cool violet healing flame, a heavenly light that cleanses and changes all situations for the better). The violet flame can help dissolve certain negative patterns or situations, helping us gain the wisdom and insight we need.

Archangel Zadkiel is said to be associated with Jupiter, the planet of luck and abundance and is known as the divine alchemist (transforming the negative into the positive). Archangel Zadkiel can often be seen holding a butterfly in his hand (one of the symbols of transformation).

Archangel Zadkiel can also help us hold fast to our truth, so we can follow our convictions by choosing the right path in life.

You can ask Archangel Zadkiel:

1) To transform your life.

2) Move forward and follow your dreams.

3) Bring luck and abundance into your life.

4) Increase your current finances.

5) Dissolve (transmute) all negative energy in your life, creating positive energy or solutions.

6) Help you to forgive.

7) Bring compassion into your life and the life of others.

8) Help you create a new beginning.

9) Feel optimistic about the future.

10) Be free from unnecessary restrictions in your life.

11) Give you the wisdom that you seek.

12) Hold fast to your convictions.

13) To keep your faith.

14) Cleanse the past and start again.

15) Be true to yourself.

16) Stay on the right path.

17) Help you feel you deserve.

18) Keep you strong.

19) Dissolve karma (past actions).

20) Give you the insight how to proceed further.

21) Attract success.

Meditation with Archangel Zadkiel
(To attract luck and Abundance into your life)

1) Find a nice space to sit or lie down (making sure your head is always supported).

2) If you can, light a candle.

3) Take three gentle breaths, inhale and exhale with each breath. Start to relax, keeping it gentle and effortless.

4) Imagine or visualise, tiny little flowers or roots coming down from the soles of your feet, pushing into the ground, spreading out into the soil below. Feel your feet strong and grounded.

5) Just relax back and call in Archangel Zadkiel, you may like to say "Archangel Zadkiel be with me now and help me attract financial security, luck and abundance into my life."

6) Get a sense or imagine Archangel Zadkiel dressed in purple robes, stepping into the room or wherever you and visualise a lovely violet light around Archangel Zadkiel.

7) Feel a sense of wisdom and support from Archangel Zadkiel.

8) Imagine Archangel Zadkiel, putting his lovely purple light around your shoulders and let this regal purple light pour around you. Let it fill every pore of your being so you feel good.

9) Explain your financial situation to Archangel Zadkiel and ask for whatever money you need. If you want your circumstances to improve and you need financial luck to come now just ask for this. Then hold a vision of Archangel Zadkiel, pouring his lovely ray of violet light into your finances and see every thing improving just getting better and better.

10) Then hold a vision of yourself as wealthy and successful, feel abundant, see yourself as happy, fulfilled, being generous and kind with all of your money, also inspiring and helping others with your successes.

11) Visualise the life you truly desire and hand your request over to Archangel Zadkiel, trust and let go.

12) Thank Archangel Zadkiel and know Archangel Zadkiel is with you now.

13) Now get a sense of yourself back from where you started from, either sitting or lying down. Visualise the little flowers or roots coming slowly up from the ground back into your feet. Your feet feel grounded and secure.

14) Slowly flex your body, stretch out if you need to. Then get up, blow out the candle and go about your day.

Affirmations and Prayers to Archangel Zadkiel:

"Archangel Zadkiel, work with me now."

"Archangel Zadkiel, be with me now."

"Archangel Zadkiel, help me attract financial security, bring abundance into my life."

"Open the way Archangel Zadkiel, so I can follow my dreams."

"Archangel Zadkiel, transform my life."

"Archangel Zadkiel, give me wisdom and insight so I can..... (explain what you need)."

"Help me move forward Archangel Zadkiel and attract success."

"Archangel Zadkiel, let me find compassion and understanding now."

"Archangel Zadkiel, show me my true path."

"Archangel Zadkiel, help me forgive…. (Describe)."

"Archangel Zadkiel, dissolve any negative energy in my life, especially to do with…… (describe the situation or person) wipe the slate clean and send a new beginning my way now."

"Archangel Zadkiel, help me stay strong in my beliefs."

"Archangel Zadkiel, open the way for luck and money to come my way."

"Archangel Zadkiel, keep me positive and optimistic now."

Remember: Thank Archangel Zadkiel, just believe, trust and let go.

The following visualisation, with Archangel Zadkiel, can help you move forward, towards transforming your life. It can help you let go of negativity, so you feel free from the past. It can help you to move on with enthusiasm, energy and vitality. It can also help you find compassion and forgiveness, showing you your true calling in this life time.

Visualisation with Archangel Zadkiel

1) Find a comfortable space to visualise in either sit or lie down, (if lying down, make sure your head is comfortable and supported).

2) Make sure the space is clear of any negative energy, use white sage or room sprays.

You might also like to work with Archangel Zadkiel's crystals (amethyst or sugalite) simply hold the crystals in your hand or have them beside you.

3) Have a candle lighting and soft music playing.

4) Breathe gently in your own time and space, inhaling and exhaling three times, feel your body start to relax.

5) Imagine tiny roots or little flowers coming down from the soles of your feet, pushing through the floor into the ground.

6) Start to visualise a ray of white light pouring into the room, see this light shining down over you from the top of your head to the bottom of your feet.

7) Breathe in this white light, let this white light fill every part of you and sense your mind becoming very wise and calm. Let your body absorb the white light and let it fill up every cell with energy and vitality.

8) Let the light fill up the space you are in, it's as if you are sitting in a circle of white divine light.

9) Call in your Guardian Angel now, you might like to say "Guardian Angel be at my side" (or whatever you feel comfortable saying) then visualise your Guardian Angel coming into the room lovingly to work with you.

10) Let your Guardian Angel, place its light and heavenly wings around you, lie back now in your angel's loving embrace.

11) When you are ready take your Guardian Angels hand and walk out of the room, imagine or visualise yourself out in nature walking thorough emerald green grass, the sun shining forming small rays of light all around you.

12) Walk through the grass following the rays of light and in the distance you see a small flat hill. You tell your Guardian Angel, that you would like to go there as you feel very drawn to the small hill or mound. Just walk to the hill now.

13) The top of the hill is quite flat and you are amazed when you reach the top, as there is a beautiful glass pyramid on the hill, radiating violet light.

14) The pyramid is big enough for you to step into, so open the glass door of the pyramid and go in with your Guardian Angel at your side. As you step inside the pyramid, there is a great feeling of peace and reverence, become aware of a lovely gentle healing sensation. Your Guardian Angel tells you, that this is the energy vibration of transformation.

15) In the centre of this pyramid, there is a beautiful purple velvet chair with soft purple cushions, a bit like a throne or regal arm chair. Sit down now in this chair and relax back. Your Guardian Angel stands beside you.

16) As soon as you sit down in this purple arm chair, you start to feel very relaxed and successful. You just know in your heart that things are about to change for the better.

17) Get a sense of a magnificent Archangel, standing in front of you dressed in purple robes, holding a violet butterfly. This is

Archangel Zadkiel and he tells you that the butterfly is a symbol of your life, which is about to transform now for the better.

18) From your heart, tell Archangel Zadkiel what you would like to change or transform in your life. Then see the butterfly fly away and know now that you are free now to create your new life with Archangel Zadkiel and all the angels help.

19) Lie back in the purple chair and let the lovely violet rays of light, from the glass pyramid wash over you.

20) If you feel, you need to forgive a person or a situation in your life, ask Archangel Zadkiel to help you now.

21) Then visualise Archangel Zadkiel putting your request, in a cool violet flame of light to be transformed, so forgiveness and compassion are now possible for everyone involved.

22) If you need to say anything else to Archangel Zadkiel, just take a few minutes to do this now.

23) Thank Archangel Zadkiel, for all his wisdom and support. Then get up from the chair, take your beloved Guardian Angel's hand, open the pyramid door and leave this beautiful violet pyramid, knowing you can return back another time.

24) Walk down the hill with your Guardian Angel, feeling completely happy. It's as if a clean slate has been offered to you, just know your life is now transforming for the better and your dreams are within reach.

25) Take your beloved Guardian Angel's hand and walk optimistically along the emerald green grass, knowing Archangel Zadkiel's violet light surrounds you now.

29) Very gently get a sense of your Guardian Angel, leading you back into the space that you started from.

30) Now visualise the little flowers or roots coming up from the ground back into the soles of your feet, your feet feel grounded and balanced.

31) Sense your upper and lower body very relaxed and breathe gently, then stretch and move your body and get up in your own time.

32) Blow out any candles and go about your day, knowing Archangel Zadkiel is at your side.

Archangel Zadkiel Story

Archangel Zadkiel has been working alongside me for many years now. I have always found Archangel Zadkiel to be a truly wonderful, compassionate and wise Archangel, who can help you to literally transform your life. I now include the following true story.

One time, I had experienced a financial set back in my life and I really needed my luck to change. I also needed guidance about where I was going in my life and what to do next.

I had been working with my angels and I had just finished reading about Archangel Zadkiel and the violet flame. I knew Archangel Zadkiel could bring you wisdom, financial assistance and even luck, helping you to transform your life in a positive loving way. So I sat down and wrote my requests out to Archangel Zadkiel. I then sat and meditated with Archangel Zadkiel working with his violet, purple light. I envisioned myself completely surrounded in this lovely violet light, as if I were sitting in a bubble of divine violet light.

Shortly after doing the meditation work, I noticed that I felt much better, much more grounded and optimistic. I started to do my laundry singing to the radio as I went about my day. I reached down to put one of my old jackets into the washing machine, when all of a sudden, a crisp new fifty euro note popped out of my jacket pocket. I was completely taken by surprise, as the note, looked perfect, not wrinkled or worn. I knew then that Archangel Zadkiel and the angels of abundance were with me. I was so delighted that I thanked Archangel Zadkiel.

Afterwards, I decided to sit in the back garden and eat my lunch, collecting my post along the way. The post had just arrived and in amongst my usual letters, was a card from my twin sister with two national lottery scratch cards enclosed. As I scratched happily away, I got a vivid sense of purple light all around me. It was as if I just knew I would win some money: and I did, I won twenty five euros on one scratch card. I was very surprised as the most I had ever won before was only four euros. So again I thanked Archangel Zadkiel, for helping me to attract luck and abundance into my life.

Later on that evening, another extraordinary thing happened, I was paying for some groceries in my local supermarket and the shop assistant at the checkout insisted that I had given her a fifty euro note, when I knew I had only given her a twenty. As I protested she insisted on giving me change for fifty euros. I definitely knew that I had only a twenty euro note in my purse, when I left the house earlier, but the checkout assistant even counted the till in front of me with the manager. Both of them were very insistent, that I was owed the money, as the till was perfectly in balance. So instead of getting just twelve euros back, I received forty two euros back.

So after a truly miraculous and transforming day, I graciously accepted the abundance that God our Creator had put my way via Archangel Zadkiel. I went home happily and then later on that night a wonderful friend of mine called to visit me, with a bottle of wine, a DVD and some Chinese food. Needless to say we had a lovely fun evening and some great chats.

The rest of my week, was really good too, amazing things started to happen; phone calls, unexpected meetings with lots of people. I even saw a course that I wanted to do and after applying for it, the money just poured in. My life seemed to transform in front of me. I felt very blessed and I knew in my heart that Archangel Zadkiel and all the angels of abundance were working with me. Thank you Archangel Zadkiel.

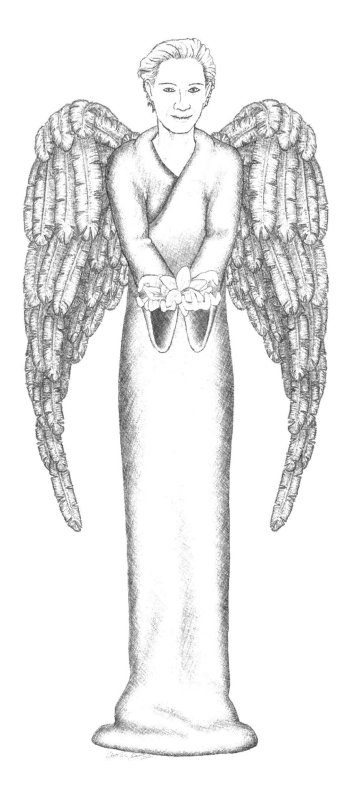

Chapter 12

Archangel Gabriel

Archangel Gabriel: is one of the principal Archangels in the heavens and is known as the heavenly awakener. The word Gabriel means: "God is my strength". Archangel Gabriel is said to be at God's left hand side and is associated with the term "Resurrection". It is said that Archangel Gabriel can resurrect any situation, giving hope and creating miracles.

Archangel Gabriel is the Archangel of communication artistic endeavours, hopes and dreams. Archangel Gabriel can make your dreams come true and deals with imagination, creativity and any artistic endeavours (writing, film, theatre, painting, singing, music etc).

Archangel Gabriel, can also help with all communication issues, especially within the family, relationships and work. Gabriel is also the Archangel associated with children, especially new born babies.

Description: Archangel Gabriel is said to wear lavender and silver robes and is often seen carrying a white lily flower, lilies being the symbol of miracles. Archangel Gabriel has a very gentle loving presence and can be associated with the moon cycles as Archangel Gabriel is the patron of the water signs (Scorpio, Pisces, cancer).

Aura: Very subtle, an almost female presence, gentle, shimmering lavender silver in colour.

Colours: Lavender, silver, lilac, sometimes soft pale blue.

Symbol: White lily flower, the moon, a star, music, bell, heavenly scroll, dreams, lavender or silver feather.

Animal: Dolphin, stork, phoenix, deer.

Crystal: Moonstone and Aquamarine.

Moonstone: is a creamy white beige transparent colour but you can also find blue moonstone as well. Moonstone can be found in tumbled or rough form and is often made into jewellery. Moonstone is associated with the moon cycles and the divine feminine. It is said to develop your intuition and known to be one of the dreaming stones. Moonstone is said to help aid with fertility issues.

Aquamarine: is a beautiful pale bluish green crystal and is said to heighten your intuition. It is also said to help heal your emotions and keep you strong. Aquamarine is often considered to be the crystal of communication and creative endeavours and is associated with the sea, dolphins, dreams and desires.

Flower Essence: *Clematis:* is said to be a wonderful little flower essence, that helps keep you focused in the present, whilst you follow your dreams and desires. It is said to enhance creativity and communication.

Working Together: Archangel Gabriel is known to be the great angelic communicator, so we can ask Archangel Gabriel to help us communicate well and express who we are.

If you are working on a creative project, you can also ask Archangel Gabriel to work with you, helping to inspire and guide your work. If you need help with your family or children, you can invoke Archangel Gabriel to work with you and your children, as Archangel Gabriel is said to the patron of children and new born babies. If you ever need a miracle in your life you can call upon Archangel Gabriel, as Gabriel is said to resurrect miracles or new beginnings into our lives.

Working with Archangel Gabriel

Archangel Gabriel is one of the main Archangels in the heavens, alongside Archangels Michael, Raphael and Uriel. Some people feel that Gabriel, is at God's left hand side, Archangel Michael at the right, Archangel Uriel is in the front and Archangel Raphael at the back.

Archangel Gabriel is the communicator (often known as the "heavenly awakener") and is said to bring hope and strength from God our Creator. Many people feel Archangel Gabriel, has a very definite but subtle presence.

Archangel Gabriel, is often seen in pale blue or lavender robes with a silver light or aura (silver is often associated with planet mercury and mercury is known as the planet of communication).

Archangel Gabriel is also the patron of all artists, dealing with the realm of the imagination and creativity. Gabriel is the Archangel to call upon, if you are involved in the arts, music, drama or writing. Archangel Gabriel can help you follow your dreams, especially if they are for your divine life purpose. If you feel you are a creative person and you want to move into the arts or write, then call upon Archangel Gabriel to guide you.

Archangel Gabriel is also considered the Archangel of new beginnings and is often associated with the moon cycles, intuition, dreaming and the divine feminine. I find a good time to work with Archangel Gabriel is at twilight, just before sunset, as the moon gets ready to appear. We are also often quite receptive and relaxed intuitively by then, as the day is over and we are preparing for the evening.

Archangel Gabriel is also said to help with all communication issues, especially within families, being the Archangel that works with all children. Gabriel can often subtly helping you with your children, and can guide you as a mother to make the right choices for your family, even helping bring in abundance for you and your family.

Archangel Gabriel is also known to work with new mothers and can often help with fertility issues, conception and birthing. Gabriel can help you name your new baby (as in biblical texts, it was Archangel Gabriel who announced to Mother Mary that she was carrying the baby named "Jesus").

Archangel Gabriel is sometimes seen carrying a "White Lily flower", which is known as the symbol of purity, hope, grace and new beginnings, bringing in miracles or to resurrect (to raise up or move forward). Lilies are often a popular flower at weddings, funerals or when someone is sick. Lilies are also a symbol of new beginnings.

I feel Archangel Gabriel can indeed "resurrect", a situation, giving us hope and creating miracles in our lives, especially if our hope is lost or we feel despondent about life. As Archangel Gabriel often works swiftly on our behalf, bringing miracles directly down from the heavenly realms.

You can ask Archangel Gabriel:

1) To resurrect a miracle in your life.

2) Help you with fertility issues.

3) Work with you as a new mother.

4) Help you name your new baby.

5) For help and support in relation to communication issues in your life.

6) Abundance for you and your family.

7) Help develop your intuition and creative imagination.

8) Help you move into the creative arts.

9) Inspire your work as a writer.

10) Help you speak your truth.

11) Balance your feminine side.

12) Guide your dreams and aspirations.

13) Help you sleep.

14) Work with the cycles of the moon.

15) Give you hope.

16) Help you make the right choices.

17) Keep your faith strong.

The following meditation, can help you connect with Archangel Gabriel, especially if you need a miracle. You can also ask Archangel Gabriel, for a miracle on behalf of someone else.

Meditation with Archangel Gabriel (For a Miracle)

1) Find a nice space to sit or lie down (make sure your head is always supported).

2) Light a candle.

3) Take three gentle breaths, inhale and exhale with each breath and now start to relax now.

4) Imagine or visualise tiny little flowers or roots, coming down from the soles of your feet pushing into the ground, spreading down into the soil below. Feel your feet safe and grounded.

5) Relax back and call in Archangel Gabriel, you might like to say "Blessed Archangel Gabriel, work with me today".

6) Then feel a lovely soft pale blue or lavender blue colour filling up the room; it seems so bright, then visualise Archangel Gabriel wearing pale blue and lavender robes with a silver glowing aura.

7) Archangel Gabriel holds a pure white lily flower, the symbol of miracles and new beginnings, just gaze into this beautiful pristine white lily flower.

8) Imagine the white lily flower as very large, with its beautiful white light pouring all around you. Breathe in its divine white light now, letting it fill your mind and body. You feel as if you are sitting in the centre of the white lily now.

9) As the white light surrounds you, talk to Archangel Gabriel. If you need a miracle simply ask Archangel Gabriel for whatever you need. If you need a miraculous solution in your life then ask Archangel Gabriel.

You might like to say: "Archangel Gabriel, send me a miracle now .....(Explain what you need)."

10) You can also ask Archangel Gabriel for a miracle on behalf of someone else.

"Archangel Gabriel send (name the person) a miracle for ... (explain the situation)."

11) Then in your own mind, hold a vision of your miracles coming about. Then visualise Archangel Gabriel just taking care of everything.

12) If this miracle is meant for you, it will come about, if not a new solution will be created anyway.

13) Then thank Archangel Gabriel and know that Archangel Gabriel is with you now.

14) Now get a sense of yourself back from where you started from, either sitting or lying down. Visualise the little flowers or roots coming slowly up back from the ground. Your feet feel very grounded and secure.

15) Flex your upper and lower body, stretch out if you need to. Blow out the candle and go about your day.

Affirmations and Prayers to Archangel Gabriel:

"Archangel Gabriel, be with me now."

"Blessed Archangel Gabriel, work with me now today."

"Archangel Gabriel, guide me in all my creative endeavours. ... (describe)."

"Dear Archangel Gabriel, help me with my fertility issues … (describe your situation)."

"Archangel Gabriel, watch over my children and help me as a mother especially with (describe)."

"Help me Archangel Gabriel, communicate better today with … (describe situation or person)."

"Archangel Gabriel, let me use my intuition wisely, enlighten and guide me now."

"Archangel Gabriel, let my dreams be beautiful and happy."

"Help me Archangel Gabriel, speak my truth; especially in relation to …(describe in detail)."

"Archangel Gabriel, send me extra financial abundance. … (describe)."

"Archangel Gabriel, keep me strong and let me have faith."

"Archangel Gabriel, remove my worries and give me clarity."

"Archangel Gabriel, help me make the right choice especially in relation to …(describe)."

"Archangel Gabriel, inspire me in all my creative pursuits."

"Archangel Gabriel, help me balance my life."

Remember: to thank Archangel Gabriel; just believe, trust and let go.

The following visualisation with Archangel Gabriel, can give you the clarity to develop your creative talents whilst staying true to yourself. It can also help you with any communication issues, helping you to speak your truth.

Visualisation with Archangel Gabriel

1) Find a comfortable space to visualise in (sit or lie down; if lying down keep your head comfortable and supported). You may also like to do this visualisation at twilight or as the sun is gently setting.

2) Make sure that wherever you are the area is positive and cleared of any negative energy. You may like to burn white sage or use a room spray.

You might also like to work with Archangel Gabriel's crystals (moonstone or aquamarine) simply hold the crystals in your hand or have them beside you.

3) Have a candle lighting and soft music playing.

4) Breathe in gently, in your own time and space, inhaling and exhaling three times and feel your body start to relax.

5) Imagine tiny little roots or little flowers coming down from the soles of your feet, pushing through the floor and spreading into the ground.

6) Start to visualise a ray of white light coming into the room, see this light pouring over you from the top of your head to the bottom of your feet.

7) Breathe in this white light, let it fill up every cell in your body and sense your mind becoming very calm.

8) Let the light continue to pour around you it's as if you are sitting in a circle of white light.

9) Call in your Guardian Angel, you may like to say "Guardian Angel be at my side" (or whatever else you feel comfortable saying) then visualise your Guardian Angel coming into the room to work with you.

10) Let your Guardian Angel place its heavenly wings around you, now lie back in your Angel's loving embrace.

11) When you are ready, take your Guardian Angel's hand and walk out of the room. Imagine or visualise yourself out in nature walking thorough emerald green grass; the sun is shining, forming small rays of light all around you.

The sky is a lovely light blue colour, breathe in this blue and feel the light breeze on your face.

12) In the distance you get a faint scent of the sea, you can almost hear the waves. Let your Guardian Angel take you by the hand now and lead to this sea shore.

13) Feel and sense the sea breeze wafting gently, that lovely fresh sea shore smell. Then take your Angel's hand and let your Angel lead you down to the beach.

14) It is such a lovely beach, the sand is a creamy white and the sea water is a gentle aquamarine colour. The sky is very blue, with soft white clouds and the sea water seems very clear with sand beneath it. You may even hear seagulls or see dolphins playing in the water. Pick up some sea shells, walk along the shore, just do whatever you feel drawn to doing.

15) Breathe in the stillness, let it fill your mind and body; after a while you realise that there is only you and your Guardian Angel on this beach. It is a heavenly beach, a sanctuary where you and your Angel can go and feel free.

16) After a while, you might decide to get into the water; the sea water is lovely and refreshing. You might even decide to swim with the dolphins that are present.

17) As you swim in the water, become very aware of three playful dolphins coming towards you, they radiate a feeling of pure joy and happiness. The dolphins swim beside you, gurgling and laughing around you. Feel their unconditional love and be very present in this moment. You might decide to swim with them if you wish.

18) You feel so good and happy in the sea with the dolphins, just absorbing this unconditional love and peace that surrounds you. The dolphins seem to intuitively know what you are thinking. Just let this goodness wash over you, feeling completely connected to all that is around you.

19) When you are ready, thank the dolphins for connecting with you today and sit back on the sea shore. Your Guardian Angel

wraps a lovely fluffy warm towel around you and the sun starts to set.

20) Become very aware now of a clear presence, with a wonderful silvery aura dressed in lavender and pale blue, just gliding on to the sand. You see a magnificent Archangel appearing carrying a white lily flower; this is Archangel Gabriel.

21) Archangel Gabriel immediately showers you with this beautiful silvery blue lavender light, from the top of your head to the bottom of your feet. You feel so good in this light, as if your natural intuitive senses have become heightened.

22) Now in your own time, have a conversation with Archangel Gabriel, a bit like an old friend; if want to become more aware about life or develop your intuitive abilities, ask Archangel Gabriel to help you.

23) If you feel you would like to develop your creative talents further or you need inspiration for your book, your painting or music, just tell Archangel Gabriel whatever you need help with. Then visualise Archangel Gabriel pouring this lovely silver blue lavender light into your request. Now hold a vision of all your dreams coming about, as you work with Archangel Gabriel.

24) If you really need to have faith in yourself and your work and hold strong to your beliefs or even to speak your truth, ask Archangel Gabriel to help you. You might like to say "Help me Archangel Gabriel, speak my truth, especially in relation to ....(describe in detail)."

25) You can also ask Archangel Gabriel, to help you with any communication issues in your life, if you need to get along

better with family, partners, or even work colleagues or if a situation needs clarity, you can simply say: "Open the way Archangel Gabriel for me to communicate better today with ….(describe situation or person)".

26) Get a sense of Archangel Gabriel, listening and working with you, even pouring this lovely silver blue light into all of your requests and prayers, know now that everything is improving. Hand it all over to Archangel Gabriel and let go.

27) Say goodbye to Archangel Gabriel, as it is twilight and the sun has set.

28) Take your Guardian Angel's hand and sense your beloved Angel leading you off the beach, walk back out into the countryside. Know Archangel Gabriel's magnificent light and support is around you now.

29) Get a sense of your Guardian Angel leading you back into the space you started from.

30) See the little flowers or roots, coming gently up from the ground back into the soles of your feet; your feet are grounded and balanced.

31) Breathe gently and flex your upper and lower body, stretch out and get up in your own time.

32) Blow out any candles and go about your day, knowing Archangel Gabriel is at your side.

The following meditation is for children, to help them meet their Guardian Angel and Archangel Gabriel. It should be recited to all children in a soft, gentle way, with relaxing music (candles and crystals are optional).

I have called **Archangel Gabriel, "Angel Gabriel"**, as it is easier for children to remember and say.

Meditation for children with Angel Gabriel

For: Parent or Teacher to recite to their children or class.

1) Find a nice place to sit down inside or sit in a circle on a nice mat (maybe in the garden).

2) Before you start, you might like to light a candle (put it in a safe place) and maybe have some aquamarine or moonstone tumble stone crystals for children to hold (tumbled crystals are far better for children, as they have more rounded edges).

Now you can start: just say: (parent or teacher).

3) "Close your eyes (only if you can) and imagine a lovely ball of white light coming into the room (or garden). As the ball of white light comes closer to you, now imagine yourself sitting in this ball of white light."

4) "Now, we will call in our Guardian Angels: Just say "My Guardian Angel come and visits me today."

5) "Imagine your Guardian Angel, putting its lovely white feathery wings, around you and giving you a big hug."

6) "Now, you and your Guardian Angel are going on a little adventure together. Go to a lovely garden with a playground.

The sun is shining its happy smile and the sky is very blue, there are also lots of lovely flowers in the garden. Other children are also playing happily in the garden beside you."

7) "In this garden, there are Angels, flower fairies and unicorns; it's a really lovely, happy, garden. Play with the Angels and fairies, and you can also even go for a ride on the back of the unicorn in the garden (wow!), just remember to have lots of fun."

8) "Beside you, the little birds are building their nests and singing their songs. Rabbits and squirrels are also playing in the garden; just say "hello" and wave to everyone in the garden."

9) "Now go over and sit on the swings, with your Guardian Angel. At the swings, there is another Angel, wearing a blue dress coming over to say "hello"; this is Angel Gabriel."

10) "Angel Gabriel smiles and gives you a white lily flower. Now give your lily flower a name, (for example say: Lucy), then thank Angel Gabriel for the beautiful white lily flower."

11) "If you have a special wish, tell Angel Gabriel, as Angel Gabriel can help make your wish come true. Quietly, Say "Angel Gabriel I would like....and say your wish"

12) "Angel Gabriel then catches your wish and puts it in a blue bubble light. Angel Gabriel tells you to blow the blue bubble with your wish inside it up to heaven. Now one, two, three... everyone blow your wish up to heaven (blowing sounds)."

13) "Your special wish now blows away, up and up to heaven it goes."

14) "Say goodbye to Angel Gabriel. "Bye bye, Angel Gabriel." Then hold your Guardian Angel's hand and go back home into your house or classroom. Feel happy and good, as it was fun meeting your Angels today".

Archangel Gabriel Story

When I work with Archangel Gabriel I always feel very inspired and supported. Archangel Gabriel often works behind the scenes, creatively observing and delivering miracles to us, when we need them the most.

Archangel Gabriel can also often help us to communicate with loved ones, past and present, especially if you need to contact someone. I had lost contact with an old friend of mine, who had returned to live back in Australia. I had tried to contact her at her old address but she had moved house. I tried everything even sending her telepathic messages via the angels, but all in vain, so I eventually gave up and handed the whole thing over to Archangel Gabriel (as I know that Archangel Gabriel can intervene in all communication issues).

About a month later, I received some redirected letters from my old flat in Dublin, to my new address in the U.K. My friend had written to me at my old address in Dublin. The amazing thing was that the letter she had written was on lavender paper with a silver pen (Archangel Gabriel's colours) on the exact day that I had asked Archangel Gabriel to help me contact her; it was truly miraculous. Thank you Archangel Gabriel.

I also know that Archangel Gabriel was instrumental in helping me write this book, as so many people, different coincidences and support was literally sent my way. Even at one stage I wasn't sure if I would actually write this book, but a friend turned up unexpectedly and gave me a bunch of white lilies along with an angel card that had a picture of Archangel Gabriel on it. So I took this as a definite sign that it was meant to be and I wrote my book. I now say a very big thank you to Archangel Gabriel for all the Angelic help and inspiration.

Chapter 13

Angel Stories

The following chapter contains completely true accounts of our Angels and how they can work with us in many different ways. These true Angel stories are from different people, family friends, clients and work colleagues. I hope these stories help and inspire you now to connect with your Angels.

A friend and colleague of mine called Mary, had been working with her Angels for many years now and one day she confided in me, that when she wants to connect to her Guardian Angel, she often recites a well known Guardian Angel Prayer that she learnt as a child (I now include this prayer).

"Oh Angel of God, my Guardian Dear"
"To whom God's love commits me here,
"Ever this day / night, be at my side,
"To light and guard,"
"To rule and guide"
"Amen."

Many people still recite this Guardian Angel prayer day and night and find great guidance from their Angels.

The following story is from Helen, who shares with us how working with her Guardian Angel and the Angels of travel have helped her.

Helen's Story

I had my first Angel session with Caroline in 2006. At this time in my life I was a bit down and I had no idea what to expect when I met Caroline, but I did have an open mind, Caroline put me at ease and straight away and I warmed to her.

We did a guided visualisation, where I got to meet my Guardian Angel, It was a truly beautiful experience and I felt so happy and calm. After it, I slept so much better, it was as if a weight was lifted off my shoulders and I could just carry on with life in the best possible way.

I am only just beginning to ask my Angels for help in all areas of my life, as until now I always thought I should only ask for little things, like finding a parking space close to wherever I needed to get to. It always seems to work for me. But last winter the ice on our roads was treacherous and as we are not on a main road our roads were not gritted. I had to travel each day and I always asked Archangel Michael and Saint Christopher to keep me safe, which they have always done and still do. Thank you Angels, and Caroline for introducing me to them.

I now include the following story as told to me by Grainne, who works as a counsellor and psychotherapist, Grainne works daily with her Angels.

Grainne's Story

In autumn of 2007, I went to Caroline as I wanted to re-connect with my Guardian Angel. I had always felt very close to my Angel, however of late my commitments had overshadowed my ability to take the time out, to work with my Angel.

Caroline did a guided visualisation with me, where I went on a spiritual journey and met my Guardian Angel. For me it was completely profound as I experienced a deep awakening and a wonderful sense of peace. I felt as if my Guardian Angel had put her wings around me in a loving embrace. I felt totally and unconditionally loved.

Since that day, I now work constantly with my Angel. I talk, and pray to her and I feel very guided and supported as My Guardian Angel always enlightens me, opening the way for my continued personal and professional growth.

As a busy counsellor and psychotherapist, I often call in my Guardian Angel to help guide me in my work and to connect with my client's Guardian Angels. As a result of doing this my counselling work is now on a completely higher spiritual level. I do feel that when I work with my Angels, the energy in the room shifts to a higher frequency and the work I do with my clients is often more direct, honest, and productive, the clients themselves also seem to move on swifter in their processes.

I now get great happiness and joy from working alongside my Angels.

I now include a wonderful Angel story, as told to me by Ethna, when she was holidaying in Spain with a friend.

Ethna's Story

I had been in Spain for about a week and I was having a really good time, the weather was great and we were staying in a lovely apartment. I was enjoying all the sights around me. One day we decided to go shopping and after looking at the shops, we went to a nice restaurant to have some lunch.

After our lunch, I decided to put on my jacket, when I realised it wasn't there. We then searched everywhere, the restaurant, the apartment where we were staying, even the shops we had visited earlier, but absolutely no luck. I especially liked that particular jacket, quite disappointed I went home.

I remembered hearing that the Angels can help you find what is lost and they can create a wonderful solution for you as well. So I asked the Angels to help me find my jacket. The next day myself and my friend were walking down a street that we hadn't gone down before and I noticed a lovely house nearby, then to my utter amazement, my jacket was hanging on the front gates of the house and it was in perfect condition.

I retrieved my jacket and I thanked the Angels. It was only afterwards that someone told me that the street where my jacket was found was called, "Street of the Angels" in English. I now know that the Angels answered my prayer that day and guided me to find my jacket.

I now include the following Angel stories from Frances, who works closely with Archangel Raphael and Mother Mary (Mother Mary has multitudes of heavenly Angels at her side).

Frances's Story

A few years ago I went to Caroline to connect with my Angels and the results were just wonderful, so many good things have happened in my life since. I now work with my Angels on a daily basis. I feel very connected to my Angels and I know that my Angels will always be there for me.

I would like to share with you now, two occasions in particular that stand out the most in my mind. About three years ago I went to Caroline, I had been given a scan in the hospital and they told me that I had quite a big cyst on my ovary and that I would need surgery. I was upset and worried. Caroline told me not to worry that the Angels would work on my behalf, if for my highest good.

We did some gentle meditation and visualisation with Archangel Raphael the Archangel of healing and I felt an incredible light pour down through my body, from the top of my head right down to the bottom of my feet. It was a gentle yet powerful divine light. Caroline was working with the white light of God our Creator and Archangel Raphael's emerald green healing light.

A couple of days later, I was scheduled for keyhole surgery. During the surgery my consultant couldn't find any trace of a cyst on my ovary. They were very surprised in the hospital, as the original scan had been so clear. I now know that Archangel Raphael and all the Angels of healing helped my cyst to dissolve easily and gently.

Another time I went to Caroline, I had just come back from Medjugorje, where I had felt very connected to Mother Mary (Our Lady). When I came home I really missed the connection I had felt with Mother Mary in Medjugorje, even though I know her presence is all around us.

I went to Caroline and we worked with the Angels, Caroline told me that Mother Mary is simply surrounded by Angels, so we asked if Mother Mary's presence could also enter into the room. All of sudden the most beautiful ray of white light came into the room, through a small window and very gently covering me. It was simple, gentle, serene and unconditionally loving. I really felt as if Mother Mary was connecting with me again through my Angels and placing her gentle cloak around me, as if to remind me that her loving presence is always with me. In truth, I just have to ask and pray to her no matter where I am.

Pauline O'Connor, a spiritual and holistic practitioner who does angel healing, reiki, reflexology and massage, explains how the Angels guided her to do the all the divine healing work she is now doing.

Pauline's Story

I went to Caroline for an Angel session in 2006. I have always had great faith in my Angels and when I went to Caroline I felt very uplifted and closely connected to my Guardian Angel and t he Archangels. Since then I now work with my Angels on a daily basis and the Angels are always working alongside me, guiding and motivating me.

The last few years, I started to feel the Angels inspiring me to start doing my holistic healing work, something I had been working on since 2003. I felt very drawn to several holistic courses and I did a reflexology course. I then felt guided to complete the course in cancer and pregnancy reflexology and I went on to study holistic massage, Indian head massage and hot stone massage.

As I come from a long line of healers, I was happy to be doing my holistic healing work. However I knew the Angels were connecting strongly with me and encouraging me to work further with them. Caroline suggested that I do an Angel course, which I did and it brought out my intuitive and healing gifts.

I now love working with the Angels and as a result of working with the Angels, I have had great healing results with all of my clients. Thank you, Angels.

I now include the following story from Orla, who told me how working with the Angels helped her to meet, her true Divine Soul-Mate and twin-flame.

Orla's Story

I came to Caroline in August 2006 for an Angel session after the failure of my second long term relationship. During the Angel session, Caroline helped me connect with Archangel Haniel and all the Angels of love, to heal my love life, so I could move forward and meet my true love.

Caroline advised me to ask Archangel Haniel and all the Angels of love, to help guide me towards meeting my true love and twin-flame (divine soul-mate). I went home that day and on the following Friday morning, I decided to write my request card out to the Angels, describing the relationship I wanted and the qualities, attributes, I desired in my partner, my twin-flame and divine soul mate. I then put my request card in an envelope, sealed it, leaving it in my Angels capable hands. I simply let go, trusting in my Angels divine guidance.

Eight months later I did meet my twin-flame (divine soul-mate) the man who was truly right for my soul, and needless to say we are both very happy now that we have met. I now work daily with my Angels, creating and manifesting the life I desire, for my highest good.

I now include this remarkable true story from Eoghan, about how our Guardian Angels and Archangels can protect and guide us, even sending earth angels (good people on the earth) into our lives.

Eoghan's Story

Shortly after I had learned to drive, I undertook a long journey. However, as this journey was longer than any other distance I had ever driven before, my wife came to support me on the long drive down. My wife had fallen asleep, in the passenger seat. After a while however, I found myself, on the wrong route. I followed the road signs directing me to the next town on our planned route home, but these signs led me down a road that was not well maintained. As I drove along this road, I searched for our original route home. I called the angels in as I drove, and as it turned out, I needed their help more than I realised.

On approaching a particular bend in the road, I slowed down. The road sign warning of a dangerous bend was obscured by trees and I didn't see it. Assuming that this bend would be the same as the rest of the road, I continued on, but the bend suddenly become sharper, and kept turning. I found myself strug- gling to stay on the road, but I had not slowed down enough and I lost control of the car, driving off the wide side of the bend, into the bushes and trees, where the car tilted up on one side, threatening to roll over.

I thought that our time had come, and I held the word "Angels" in my mind, as a silent plea for help. The car landed back onto its wheels on the road, and bounced across the road, over a wall of stones, and into the field on the inside of the bend. Here we came to rest, balanced on a pile of stones that had fallen from the wall.

With the car now stopped, fear set in, as I realised what had happened. Miraculously, my wife and I were mostly unhurt apart from some bruising on my wife's arm and leg. We emerged from the car to examine our situation. We barely had time to look at where we were, when another car pulled up on the side of the road that we had just left.

A man dressed in blue got out and jumped into the field beside us. He calmly reassured us that all would be fine, and he examined our situation. The engine of my car was fine, but the stones had suspended it above the ground. The man drove his car up to mine, tied a rope between the cars, and freed my car from the stones.

With our lives intact, and our car drivable, my wife and I could then see our way out now. The helpful stranger said that it was a miracle we were unhurt. He had never seen people walk away unharmed from a crash like that, and told us we were very lucky, that the car didn't turn over. "It obviously wasn't your time to go" he said. We were then able to drive the rest of the way home in our car, although still quite shaken.

I truly believe that the angels were protecting my wife and me that day. Considering the severity of the crash, the fact that my wife and I were without serious injury was a true miracle. For our car to be in any condition to drive us home was also amazing. For the man (we will call him "B") to arrive when he did, and for him to know exactly what to do, was true Angelic aid, sent to us when we needed it the most.

There were so many small factors, that could have conspired to make this crash a more tragic event, but it was more than luck that kept us safe. I thank the angels daily for our good health in walking away from that accident.

Andrea Conboy, now relays how the Angels work alongside her in many different ways, as an holistic therapist.

Andrea's Story

The angels mean so much to me, I ask for their help every day and I know that I always have the Angels to turn to, even in the most difficult and confusing situations. They always guide me in the right direction whether I realise it or not at the time.

Since working with my Angels, my outlook on life has changed so much, as the Angels have helped me beat a stress related illness and they have helped me to do the work I love. I know I can put my worries into their hands and everything will work out.

I am a massage therapist holistic practitioner and spa manager, and I have seen real miracles happen when I've asked Archangel Raphael to help clients out with some of their problems. I always trust in the Angels to help me find my way forward and show me the truth.

At one point in my life I was having doubts as to whether I was going in the right direction with my work. I had aspirations to do something more challenging, but didn't know how to go about it. The angels guided me to plan out the career I wanted and amazingly all the right opportunities presented themselves exactly as I had imagined. I have faith that I am on the right path now, exactly where I'm meant to be, with the angels guiding my every step.

My life is so much more positive, healthy and fulfilling, because the Angels are in my life. I am grateful to Caroline, for showing me how to connect with my Angels. As I now know, that I can work with the Angels myself, anytime, anywhere and they will always help me in the best way they can.

I now include the following story from Emer Hennelly who works as a massage therapist and counsellor psychotherapist.

This is a wonderful example of how the angels can guide you to find your true divine work.

Emer's Story

The first time I had an angel healing with Caroline was in 2006. I was at a huge crossroads in my life and I was very uncertain about many aspects of my life. It was a frustrating and fearful time for me. Then I was introduced to Caroline and I had the most wonderful angel healing session. I told Caroline that I was thinking of training in holistic massage, but I was unsure if this was the right thing to do.

Caroline told me not to worry and just to put it out there and ask the angels for guidance, and that I would receive a clear sign if this career choice was meant to be for me. About three days later, I opened the paper and there was a large advertisement for a massage training course. I knew this was a clear sign from my angels and I decided to do the course. Since then I have had a complete career change, as I did the massage training course and I then went on to train as a grief counsellor and psychotherapist.

I now connect regularly with my angels and as a result of working with the angels my life has unfolded in a much more positive and fulfilling way.

It's wonderful to be able to work with my angels now and to receive the necessary angelic help and guidance in my life, whenever I ask. I am so grateful to the angels for helping me to do the work that I love.

Vivian tells the following story of how Archangel Michael and all the Angels of protection worked with her, at a very important time in Vivian's life.

Vivian's Story

In 2008, I was facing a very serious court case, where I was fighting for the safety and protection of my three and half year old daughter. I was told by solicitors that the Judge would never grant, what I asking for and that the Judge never gave anyone enough time, to explain their side of the story in court. It looked very bleak and I was very worried.

So I contacted Caroline and I booked an Angel appointment. During the Angel session, we invoked Archangel Michael and all the Angels of protection and justice. Caroline also told me to work with the Angels myself at home and to write my Angel request prayer to them. Then to visualise the Angels creating the best possible result for everyone involved.

After my Angel session I felt very strong and protected, as if an extra layer of support was placed around me from my Angels. I went home and wrote my prayer request out to the Angels, then I simply let it go and I trusted that all would be well.

The outcome of the court case was truly miraculous. The Judge really did listen to me and gave me as much time as I needed to talk. She (the Judge) also ruled in my favour and granted all my wishes. My solicitor was simply amazed that day but I definitely knew that the court room was filled up with Angels.

That experience gave me back my faith in life and helped me to trust in all that is good and loving. I now know that speaking your truth and working from your heart, is the best possible way to move forward whilst staying in the light of God and the Angels. It made me realise that we can ask the Angels for any help when we need it and that the Angels will always hear our call for help and work with us. I feel now that at anytime, I can simply connect to my Angels to help improve and transform my life and the lives of others, in a positive, light filled way.

I feel very blessed to have had this miracle and to have met Caroline, who helped me connect to my Angels again, whilst sharing her wisdom, intuitive knowledge and guidance with me.

I now include several true stories, as told to me by well known life and personal development coach, Marguerite Dolan-Langan. Marguerite explains how working with the Angels brought harmony and support into all areas of her life.

Marguerite's Stories

My work involves working with large groups and individuals. I am blessed to be doing the work I truly love and I love doing it. However there are times when jumping from one group to another, can bring my energy down, so I need to help keep the energy positive to meet the needs of the people I am working with.

I was about to start with a new group of 18 that were fairly young in age. Early on that first morning, I had some time, so I sat quietly and lit a white candle, asking my Angels and guides to be with me, to allow me to meet the needs of those I would be working with.

I then asked for the Angels of every member, in the group to join in, helping to highlight the needs of each person, with whom I would work with that day. The results were amazing, the classroom glowed with light, and even though I continued to talk, there was a still silence around the room, and every student had a soft white glow all around them.

I was amazed, I stopped talking for a moment to feel the presence in the room, it was so hard to describe, it was like everybody in the room was keenly alert open, smiling, totally attentive and wrapped up in the process. Not wanting to disturb this magical powerful presence, but needing to check in with the students, I quietly asked "was everyone okay" the replies came in tones of quiet, with nods and smiles, asking me to continue.

The feeling and energy of this group remained the same throughout out the course. I now continue to ask for help from my own angels, and I also invite the angels of my clients and students to be present when I am working. When these precious moments happen, which they do time and time again, I am always grateful and totally amazed.

There have been also many times in my life, when I call on my Angels for protection and guidance and they have always been there for me. I usually feel their presence. On one occasion I even heard them and I sometimes see my Angels. My family know of my love for my Angels and when they are concerned for me travelling alone (which I do for my work) I would always let them know however, I was perfectly safe. I am never alone, sometimes the car is totally full with my travelling angels. I feel I wouldn't even have room for another passenger.

One particular evening shortly after the sudden death of a family member, I was travelling home late in the evening. It was with great sadness and a heavy heart that I drove the car that night, the journey would take about an hour to do. My mobile rang with a call from my brother, who knew I was on the road and was concerned, as he knew I was travelling alone, and as we all were very sorrowful during this time, he was not very happy that I was on the road that late at night.

After he had finished talking, he just started laughing, and said "I suppose you are going to tell me that the car is full to capacity with your Angels"? Just as he said this, the back seat of the car filled up, I could feel three large Angels sitting very joyfully, happy to be there, along for the road trip, although I could not see them, I felt their love, support and joy. I told my brother, I was in good and safe company and not to worry. I ended the call to my brother with the promise to ring him when I got home.

What I omitted to tell him, was the Angels had brought our recently deceased family member with them, who sat in the front seat, his presence filled up all the space, and I could hear him tell me that he would travel part of the journey with me, and he did.

My three loving Angels in the back seat, as I travelled, held my sadness that evening, to this day I still feel their loving support.

I now work with my Angels daily, and over the last few years, I am very happy to have worked with Caroline, who has helped me connect strongly to my Angels.

Chapter 14

Conclusion

I hope, after reading this book and working with your Guardian Angel and the Archangels, you now feel more connected to your angels. Just know that you can call upon your angels at any time and they will always work on your behalf, you only have to ask.

As I have said before angels are there for everyone regardless of belief or background. So if you feel happy lighting a candle and connecting to the angels in your own space then that is wonderful. Or if you prefer sitting out in nature or in a church or temple, then that is fine to. It's really whatever works best for you at the time.

The angels will always come to you regardless of where you are. Again there really is no separation, as we are all the same in the eyes of God our Creator. Sometimes certain belief systems choose to isolate people, creating fear based thinking and prejudices, but this is really a negative form of thinking, as it often creates ego and power struggles, especially when people start to think they are better than others. This way of thinking is not from God, as God our Creator is always eternally loving and forgiving.

So when things become simply too much for us as human beings, we can always seek solitude in our heavenly angel's loving embrace. Once you have connected with the angels you will always be with them, for their love and constant support is never ending.

There have been many, many times in my life, that the angels have literally moved mountains for me. Especially when I have had insurmountable obstacles to overcome, somehow the angels always cleared them for me, letting the sun shine back into my life.

You will find the more you work with the angels, the more peaceful your life will become and you will feel less inclined to worry or fret. You will also seem more drawn to nature, healing and learning and you will start to connect with positive people; life will just seem happier with each day that beckons forward.

If something doesn't happen in the way you want, when you work with the angels, remember it might not be in your best interest, or something better may occur in the long term. There were times in my own life, when I didn't always receive instant results, as I had to wait a bit longer. But I was always grateful for the particular journey it took me on, especially the life knowledge, I learned along the way which helped me at a later stage in my life.

An example of this, can often be wishing for a certain person or relationship, when God and the angels may have someone better for you, waiting in the wings. The important thing is to trust in the angels' guidance and believe that the right solution is forthcoming.

Remember, that we are all part of this life on the earth and everything around us is connected. So one action does affect another (some people call this the "law of Karma" or "reaping what you sow"). It really doesn't matter the label, what's important is that we all move forward together now, in a positive, loving, way, doing the best we can for ourselves and others.

Our Angels are indeed loving, light filled heavenly messengers that are created in the mind of God our Creator. So please do call them in and work with them; then watch as simply wonderful blessings and miracles start to fill up your life.

Angel-hugs and blessings to you all,

Caroline Quigley.

About the Author

Caroline Quigley is an Irish Author, Intuitive, Healer, and a twin, and is originally from County Wicklow, in Ireland.

Caroline was born with natural intuitive abilities and has been connecting to the heavenly angels and spiritual world, ever since she was a young child.

Caroline initially began her working life in the arts (theatre and film). Then in 1997, Caroline experienced a very profound healing experience that reconnected her back to the Angelic realm. As a result of this experience, Caroline's natural intuitive and healing gifts began to heighten, prompting Caroline to study healing and holistic medicine.

Caroline completed a spiritual healing course and several angel courses, A creating with angels diploma course (A.M.A.N.F.), advanced angel ritual course, masters certificate (M.M.A.N.F.) also flower essences (BSYA F.Ess) and healing meditation (BSYA H.Md) diplomas.

In 2008 Caroline started writing and wrote An Angel Calling, her first book, which was then published in 2011. Caroline has also written two accredited distant learning courses, Angel Healing and Celtic Angels for the BSY College Group in the UK, also a children's Angel book, Angel Cards and a meditation cd.

In June 2013, Caroline wrote her first teen young adult, fantasy adventure novel, Phoenica Rising - Keeper of Light, part of a trilogy series. Caroline is also working on a new Celtic book of Poems and various inspirational short stories.

Most of Caroline's books are inspired by her own experiences and the beautiful natural landscape of the Burren in the West of Ireland.

Printed in Great Britain
by Amazon